# NARADIYA DHARMASASTRA

OR

# THE INSTITUTES OF NARADA

# NARADIYA DHARMASASTRA

OR

# THE INSTITUTES OF NARADA

TRANSLATED, FOR THE FIRST TIME, FROM THE UNPUBLISHED SANSKRIT ORIGINAL

BY

DR. JULIUS JOLLY,

UNIVERSITY, WURZBURG

WITH A PREFACE, NOTES CHIEFLY CRITICAL, AN INDEX OF QUOTATIONS FROM NARADA IN THE PRINCIPAL INDIAN DIGESTS, AND A GENERAL INDEX.

GYAN

*Published by*

GYAN

Gyan Publishing House
5, Ansari Road
Daryaganj, New Delhi-110002
Phone: 011-47034999, 9811692060
E-mail: books@gyanbooks.com

*Distribution Network*
gyanbooks.com
India, USA, Canada, UK, Australia, France



ISBN : 978-81-212-2838-1 (HB)
First Published, 1876

2nd Impression 2021

*Printed at:* Gyan Press, Delhi.



**Naradiya Dharmasastra**
Author: Dr. Julius Jolly

# NÁRADÍYA DHARMASÁSTRA,

OR

# THE INSTITUTES OF NÁRADA.

TRANSLATED, FOR THE FIRST TIME, FROM THE UNPUBLISHED SANSKRIT ORIGINAL

BY

DR. JULIUS JOLLY,

UNIVERSITY, WÜRZBURG.

*WITH A PREFACE, NOTES CHIEFLY CRITICAL, AN INDEX OF QUOTATIONS FROM NÁRADA IN THE PRINCIPAL INDIAN DIGESTS, AND A GENERAL INDEX.*

LONDON:

TRÜBNER & CO., LUDGATE HILL.

1876.

RESPECTFULLY DEDICATED

TO

SIR HENRY SUMNER MAINE. K.C.S.I., LL.D.,

MEMBER OF THE COUNCIL OF INDIA, AND PROFESSOR OF JURISPRUDENCE IN THE UNIVERSITY OF OXFORD,

BY THE

EDITOR.

# PREFACE.

The *Náradíya Dharmaçástra* or Náradasmṛiti, like most of the Smṛitis, or ancient codes of revealed law of the Hindus, is called by the name of an ancient Ṛishi, and his authorship is expressly stated in the introduction, but it requires no proof that Nárada, "the divine sage," a well-known legendary personage and reputed author of some hymns of the Rigveda, cannot be its real author.

Not even our work itself, or epitome, as the introduction defines it, supports this view; on the contrary, Nárada is quoted as an old authority, Ch. v, 111, exactly in the same way as the authoritative sayings of Manu are quoted in other places. The introduction, on the other hand, is clearly a later addition, and its secondary origin is even more apparent than is the case with the introductory chapters, or passages, prefixed to the Manu, Yájnavalkya, and Vishṇu Smṛitis, as it is written in prose, whereas the work itself (except ch. ii, 24, where a different metre occurs) consists of continuous Çlokas.

Who, then, was the real author of the Institutes of Nárada, and to what period does this work belong? The former question can only be answered in a very general way; it may be taken for granted, that is to say, that the metrical version of this law-book is the work of some learned Brahmin, who brought an old prose work on law, which may have borne the same title, into its present shape; but who that versifier was and how far he altered his original, is not likely ever to be discovered.

Turning immediately to the second question, therefore, I shall examine what conclusions as to the age of the present work may be drawn from internal and circumstantial evidence, and, especially, from a comparison with the rest of the Smṛitis.

These old law-works may be divided into two principal classes,* viz.,

i. Dharma- or Sámayáchárika-Sútras.

* See Weber and Stenzler in Weber's "Indische Studien," i, 57, 69, 143, 232, Max Müller, in a letter printed in Morley's Digest, i, p. cxcvi, note (wherein the origin of Manu's law-code is discussed), the same in his Hist. of Anc. Sanskr. Lit. pp. 86, 99, 133, and, particularly, Bühler in his Introduction to the Bombay Digest, edited by him and West. Bühler's views have been adopted and confirmed by Burnell, Pref. to Dâyavibhâga (Madras 1868), p. vi, and Weber, "Indische Streifen," ii, pp. 404–8, "Indische Literaturgeschichte," 2nd. ed. (Berlin, 1876) p. 296, nt.

*i.e.* literally "Aphorisms on law or established custom," written partly in prose, partly in mixed prose and verse.

ii. Metrical versions of such works.

Specimens of the former class are: Ápastamba's Dharmasútra, edited by Bühler, and the Dharmasútra bearing the name of Vishṇu. The chief works of the latter class are: the Institutes of Manu, of Yájnavalkya, of Paráçara, and the present work.

Now this classification has a historical value also, the works of the first class being, generally speaking, older than those of the second class.

That the Institutes of Nárada belong to a later period than the *bulk* of any of the Dharmasútras—for some of them are full of subsequent additions—can be proved, even if we are prepared to admit that the composition of prose works in the Sútra style had not entirely ceased when the composition of metrical Smṛitis began. The mere fact that our work is expressly a law treatise, whereas in *all* the other Smṛítis jurisprudence is mixed up with a vast deal of extraneous matter, as *e.g.*, disquisitions on the creation and the four ages of the world, the twenty-one hells, transmigration, and final beatitude, rules of purification and diet, of penance, and expiation of crimes, and such like theòlogical speculations and moral precepts, goes very far to prove the posterior origin of the former. The separation of moral precepts from laws is everywhere, and especially among such a religious nation as the Hindus, the work of a comparatively late period. And to this it must be added, that not only is the law merged in foreign matter in the other works, and especially in the Dharmasútras, but that little importance is attached to it by them, which is shown by the fact that it meets with a very insufficient treatment there. Thus the Vishṇusútra has only 6 chapters on laws properly speaking (viz., ch. v, vi, xv, xvii, xviii, xxiv), out of a hundred chapters, of which the whole work consists, to put side by side with the 18 Vyavahárapadas of our work. A similar conclusion to that drawn from these general considerations has been reached by comparison of a single, but highly important, branch of law, as treated in the Dharmasútras of Vishṇu, Vasishtha, Ápastamba, Gautama, and Baudháyana, with the corresponding sections in Nárada's, Manu's and Yájnavalkya's Dharmaçástras. A careful analysis, namely, of the texts *on inheritance* from the six first-mentioned authors, as printed in the 1st volume of the Bombay Digest, and of Manu's and Yájnavalkya's rules on the same subject, as contained in the editions of these authors, has led A. Mayr to the conclusion, that Nárada—I retain this name for convenience' sake—must be younger than the Dharmasútras mentioned, and not only than these, but also than Manu and Yájnavalkya.* There are other points of at least equal importance, which confirm the latter view, and to these I have now to advert, leaving aside the minor metrical Dharmaçástras, as

* Aurel Mayr, "Das indische Erbrecht" (Wien, 1873) pp. 5, nt. 1, 48, 59, 62, 77, etc.

being mostly of no significance whatever, and being, likewise, most of them, even the celebrated Dharmaçástra of Paráçara, no law-books in the proper sense of the term.

As regards *Manu,* in the first place, it is well known that the native tradition considers him as the first of lawgivers and the fountain-head of jurisprudence; and there is no reason to contradict this opinion, as regards the original version of his code, until a strict examination of the Mánava Gṛihyasútra, which appears to have been recently discovered, will have proved its fallacy (compare Weber's Ind. Literaturgesch., l. c.). If, indeed, we were to believe the author of the Introduction to Nárada, this very work would be the remainder of part of an old epitome in 12,000 Çlokas from the original code of Manu, and consequently older, as far as it goes, than that form of it which we now possess, the latter being, according to the same source, only an epitome of the former epitome, made in a subsequent period by Sumati. Apart from the mythical ingredients of this statement, which, following the example of Sir W. Jones in the Pref. to his translation of M., p. xx, we might overlook, and apart from the doubtful authority from which it comes, there is nothing incredible in it *a priori*; but on a closer examination and comparison of the two works in question, three reasons at least become apparent, which make the alleged relation between Manu and Nárada highly improbable.

*Firstly,* this author has but a very limited number of

Çlokas in common with Manu, as will be seen from the list of quotations in the Appendix. The Vishṇu-smṛiti, which has nothing at all to do with Manu, has yet a far greater number of Çlokas in common with him than the Náradasmṛiti.

*Secondly,* there exists no trace of a different and more bulky version of our work.

If a Náradasmriti in twelve thousand Çlokas had ever been in existence, we should no doubt find some quotations from it here and there, just as a *Vṛiddha Manu* and a *Bṛihan Manu* are often quoted in later works, and as indeed of almost every Smriti several versions, called respectively *bṛihat* "large," or *laghu* "little," and *vṛiddha* "old" are quoted, and some of them are actually in existence.

Of the Náradasmṛiti, on the other hand, as far as I know, no *bṛihat,* nor indeed any other version than the one here translated,* is ever quoted.

* I have met with two quotations from a Bṛihannáradíya in Nandapaṇḍita's Vaijayantí, the celebrated commentary on the Vishṇusútra, one of them (MSS. of the I. O. L. 915, f. 131, b, 6), containing an enumeration of the spirituous liquors prohibited to members of the four higher classes and to women; the other (ibid. f. 146, b, 8) stating some exceptions to the well-known custom of Suttee, viz. in cases of pregnancy, suspected pregnancy, and so forth. These passages, occurring as they do in a work on law, might have been taken from the *áchára* section of a more copious version of Nárada. But the first passage being addressed to an assembly of "excellent Dvijas" (dvijottamáḥ), and the second (which has been translated, without the source being mentioned, in Colebrooke's Essay on the 'Duties of a Faithful Hindu Widow,' Ess. i, 138), to a princess, the daughter of Ságara, there can be little doubt, that the term Bṛihannáradíya

That the activity of the unknown author of our work did not confine itself to a mere epitomising of some larger and older redaction of Manu, can be shown, *thirdly*, by a comparison of its contents with those of *our* Manu, and such a comparison will at the same time afford much help in deciding the chronological question.

Bühler has already called attention to the discrepancies between the two authors as to the number and manner of ordeals, the enumeration of the heads of dispute, and the permissibility of the Niyoga, or appointment of a widow by her relations to raise offspring to her deceased lord. The last point is of no importance, as the prohibition of the Niyoga, Manu ix, 64–68, which immediately follows the rules as to its application, is clearly an interpolation, made in a period when this patriarchal custom had fallen into desuetude.* As regards the heads of dispute, or titles of law, their number is the same in both authors, and the difference relates more to the names and to the arrangement than to the matter, though it is characteristic that Manu enumerates two more titles relating to criminal laws than Nárada (*steyam* and *strísaṅgrahanam*), and that Nárada's last head of dispute, or title of law, is denominated "Miscellaneous Disputes" or "Sundries."

in both cases refers to the Bṛihannáradíyapuráṇa, which is occasionally quoted in this abbreviated form, v. Böthlingk-Roth's Dictionary, s. v.

* Cf. the general note appended to Sir W. Jones' translation of the code of Manu. Even Yájnavalkya (i, 68, 69), who is decidedly younger than Manu, sanctions the custom of Niyoga, and so do all the other authors of *ancient* Smritis.

The introduction of such a title as this is the sign of an expansion of the original limits of the legislation;* the predominance of the criminal laws over the civil, on the other hand, is always indicative of an early stage of jurisprudence. But no other point of difference proves so distinctly the high antiquity of Manu as the isolated position which he holds among the lawgivers as to the administration of ordeals. This point has been already brought out by Stenzler in an essay, "Uber die indischen Gottesurtheile," and to his observations it may be added, as far as Nárada is concerned, 1st, that he knows both forms of the administration of an ordeal, that mentioned by Manu, as test of an oath (Nár. 5, 104=Manu, 8, 115), and that mentioned by the rest of the lawgivers, as a proof of innocence; 2ndly, that Nárada mentions not only five kinds of ordeals, *i.e.*, three more than Manu, but that besides the five kinds expressly described by him, ch. v–ix, he must have known (6.) the chewing of grains of rice, and (7.) the taking out of a piece of gold from hot oil. Distinct allusions to these two kinds of ordeals, of which a later author, Pitámaha, gives a detailed description, are found in Nár. ch. ix, 8; i, 16.

The points noticed by Bühler, and the different treatment of the Law of Inheritance in both works, as pointed out by Mayr, are, however, far from being the only discrepancies between Manu and Nárada. The

* Cf. Stenzler's remarks in the excellent Essay above referred to, Ztschr. d. d. morg. Ges. ix, 678.

systematizing spirit which characterises the whole Hindu legislation is only seen in its germs in the code of Manu, but it is fully developed in Nárada. Thus the latter enumerates three kinds of property only instead of the seven or ten mentioned by Manu, but he subdivides each again into seven species; the fourfold division of the law of gift with its thirty-two subdivisions is peculiar to Nárada, who also distinguishes between fifteen forms of slavery, whereas Manu knows but of a sevenfold division of bondage; Nárada's curious division of impotent persons into fourteen sorts is not found in Manu, nor, indeed, in any other law-book. He names twenty-one descriptions of women, with whom an incest may be committed, and three kinds of abuse, to which he assigns special denominations. Instead of Manu's prohibition *pure et simple* of every kind of game, we find public gaming-houses mentioned, and elaborate rules as to their administration laid down, in Nár. ch. xvi; etc. etc. In the first part, on judicature, his enumeration of incompetent witnesses is far more comprehensive than Manu's: of all those classifications regarding jurisdiction, ordinary and appellate, the four parts of a judicial proceeding, etc., which the first chapter of Nárada contains, Manu has only the abovementioned division of the titles of law into eighteen heads. And to those points of difference between this division and Nárada's eighteen heads of dispute, which have been noticed above, it has to be added, that Manu confines himself to a simple enumeration of the eighteen titles in the introductory part of the section on judicature and laws (viii, 4–7; cf. ix, 250), and does not, in the enumeration of the laws themselves, bind himself strictly to the order observed in enumerating the titles of law. It is easy to see that almost all these points of difference do not merely relate to the outward form of the laws, but are such as to show that the spirit as well as the form of the legislation is at a later stage of development in Nárada than in Manu. Take, for instance, the different treatment of the laws regarding gambling and betting. It is true, that the native commentators, as usual, try to explain this difference away, as the texts of the lawgivers, being based on revelation, according to their theory, cannot be at variance with one another. Mitramiçra, in the Víramitrodaya (p. 721 of the new Calc. ed.), informs us that Manu's prohibition of gambling and betting relates to such cases only, where false dice are used, or the permission of the king has not been obtained. The latter interpretation is given in the Vyavahára-mayúkha also (v. Stokes' H. L. B. p. 165), and from a saying of Vṛihaspati, quoted in the Víramitrodaya, ibid., and in the Vivádachintámani (p. 166 of the Calc. ed.), we may gather, that even this old lawgiver had already noticed the glaring difference between the code of Manu and the rest of the Smṛitis on the point in question, and had attempted a third mode of explanation for it. Thus he fully approves Manu's prohibition on the one hand, because truth, purity, and fortune are destroyed by gambling; but, on the other hand, he concurs as heartily with the opinion of other legislators, who approve of gaming-houses superintended by Government, because they assist the police in finding out thieves.* A new reason indeed for the toleration of gambling. All these artificial theories are superseded by the simple assumption that the code of Manu was composed at a time when the evil consequences, with which the inveterate and truly national passion for gambling was attended, had made themselves generally felt, but when the ingenious device of making one of the worst propensities of the subjects a source of income for the sovereign, had not yet struck the minds of Hindu legislators. As it is in this case, so it is in all the rest; the only way to account for the discrepancies between Manu and Nárada is by taking the latter author to have lived considerably later than the former. This is quite manifest also in the case of the rules on judicature, which are as primitive as possible in Manu, but fully developed in Nárada.

The pre-eminent importance of the code of Manu made it necessary to treat its relation to the present law-book as fully as the limits of a preface would allow; but I shall be as brief as possible with regard to the relative antiquity of Nárada and Yájnavalkya. It becomes, indeed, apparent, from a mere general survey of the latter code, that it must be younger than Manu's, but earlier than Nárada's, and in most

* Compare the rules regarding the inquiry after thieves and murderers, Manu ix, 258-261; Yájnavalkya ii, 267; Nárada xiv, 18.

of the abovementioned points in particular, occupies an intermediate position between them. Thus Yájnavalkya knows five kinds of ordeals, but the description he gives of them is extremely short.* He is one of those lawgivers who sanction gambling, if it is superintended by the king, or his officers; but Nárada mentions a greater number of games and gives more detailed rules as to their supervision than he. And if, on the one hand, the law of commerce is quite, and the judicatory nearly, as much developed as in Nárada's Institutes, the latter work, on the other hand, is far more methodical and systematic than that of Yájnavalkya, who does not even know the eighteen titles, nor indeed any other classification of the laws. Buddhism, finally, is nowhere mentioned in Nárada, but quite distinctly alluded to in Yájnavalkya †; and if this important *argumentum a silentio* has been deservedly used by some as a proof of antiquity in the case of Manu, it may be used with at least the same force as a proof of a comparatively recent date in the case of

* It is not unlikely that Nárada's description of the ordeals, as contained in the MSS., is a mere extract from a more copious discussion of the same subject, v. p. 45, nt. 2. But, even in its present form, this section is far more comprehensive than the corresponding one in Yájnavalkya's code.

† See Stenzler's preface to his Yájnavalkya. Such general expressions as *nástika* "atheist," *naigama*, a sectary who detracts from the authority of the Vedas (according to some; according to others, "citizen"), *páshaṇḍa* "heretic." Nár. ch. v, 37. x. head of dispute, 1, 2, *pravrajitá*, "female ascetic," xii. h. of d., 74, cannot be regarded as containing allusions to adherents of Buddha.

Nárada, so that it can at no rate be fixed at an earlier time than the rise of Buddhism.

Thus our law-book must have been composed or brought into its present shape at a time when the faith of Buddha had not merely begun to succumb to the victorious assaults of the Brahmins, but when it had been completely replaced by the old Brahminical system. It may be added, that the opinion here expressed as to the relative antiquity of Yájnavalkya and Nárada is not only confirmed by Mayr's investigations on the Law of Inheritance, but also by the authority of Stenzler, who takes none of the other lawgivers except Manu to have been prior to Yájnavalkya.

The two facts, that the Institutes of Nárada must be of later date than those of Manu and Yájnavalkya, and that they must have been composed decidedly after the beginning of the Brahminical reaction against Buddhism, help us to fix their earliest possible date at about 400 or 500 A.D. It is certain, on the other hand, that our work must be much older than the Mitáksharà, which frequently quotes it, together with most of the other Smṛitis. For though the composition of such works may in one or two cases have extended to the tenth century A.D.,* such learned compilations as the Mitáksharà, which could only be understood by a very few, are separated by a wide gulf from the simple, though laconic, *versus memoriales* of the metrical Smṛitis. Now the author of the

* Burnell, Introduction to Dáyavibhága, p. vii.

Mitákshará, Vijnáneçvara, has been shown by Bühler * to have lived in the second half of the 11th century A.D.; and if we take the latest of the numerous Sṛmitis quoted by him to be two centuries earlier, we should arrive at the latter half of the ninth century as the latest possible date of our work. But it may be safely asserted, although the majority of those Smṛitis can only be judged now by fragments, that Nárada is much rather one of the oldest, than one of the youngest of them. Thus a comparison of his work with the many passages quoted from the detailed works of Kátyáyana and Vṛihaspati in the Mitákshará and other Law Digests, will readily convince every one that our work must be older than these; in the case of the Pitámaha, Yama and Vyása Smṛitis, the same conclusion will be reached, not only from similar reasons like these, but also from the fact that these Smṛitis cannot but be results of Çankara's teaching.† If, therefore, our work is placed intermediately between the ninth and second centuries A.D., the latter period being according to Stenzler the earliest possible date of Yájnavalkya, the fifth or sixth century would be the probable time of its origin. Perhaps this date is somewhat too early, as Yájnavalkya is more likely to have lived after than before 200 A.D., and as Nárada must be one or two centuries younger than Kumárila, the first champion of the Brahmins in their victorious struggle against Buddhism. The materials of our work are of course much older, and many of

* Note on the age of the Mitáksharà. Bombay, 1868.

† Burnell l. c. ix.

the laws it contains belong to the remotest antiquity.

No printed edition of the Sanskrit text existing as yet, the section on Inheritance (xiii. head of dispute) excepted, which has been edited and translated by Bühler in the 1st vol. of the Bombay Digest, this version has been made chiefly from two MSS., L= Sanskrit MSS. of the I. O. L. London, No. 1300, and B=MSS. orient. fol. 496 of the Berlin Library, which were kindly lent me by the Chief Librarians of these two Libraries. Both MSS. are quite modern, the former being dated Saṃvat 1857, and the latter, which is among the most recent acquisitions of the Berlin Library and not contained in Weber's Catalogue, being written on blue letter-paper. These two MSS. are derived from the same *Codex archetypus*, to which L stands nearer than B; yet the cases are not quite rare in which the latter MS. helps to restore the original reading, as both MSS. contain a great number of clerical errors, which are only here and there corrected. In some cases the text is so strongly corrupted in both MSS. as to be quite unintelligible; in one case (ch. ii. 8 b–11) three Çlokas and a half are omitted in B, and both MSS. have omitted several Çlokas or hemistichs in various places; nor are the interpolations wanting, which the carelessness of the Lekhaks of India in inserting marginal notes into the text they are copying, is so apt to occasion.*

* v. Bühler, Critical Introduction to Ápastambíyadharmasútram I (Bombay, 1868), p. 7. Perhaps the repetitions noticed in the

Under these circumstances I have been glad to avail myself very largely of the help which the exceedingly numerous quotations from the Smṛitis in the mediæval Law Digests and Commentaries afford to an editor and translator of these old works. It will be seen from the index of quotations in the Appendix, that *upwards of half* the 850 Çlokas or thereabouts, of which this work consists, have been traced in the Law Digests and Commentaries, not to mention some others that have been traced in Manu.

Those works are: *a*, of Sanskrit texts, Vijnáneçvara's Mitáksharâ, the Víramitrodaya of Mitramiçra, the Vivádachintámani of Váchaspatimiçra, and some of Raghunandana's Tatvas; *b*, of the English translations of such works, the Sanskrit text of which is not printed, or was not within my reach: Jagannátha's Digest, translated by Colebrooke, and the Vyavahára-mayúkha, translated by Borrodaile, the latter work, however, containing but a very few quotations that are not contained in the other law-books also.*

These quotations have proved equally useful for supplying omissions, for tracing interpolations, and for making corrections; and but for the invaluable aid I derived both from them and from the comments frequently attached to them, this translation would probably never have been undertaken.

enumeration of incompetent witnesses, p. 37, are also due to such interpolations.

* Kullúka's gloss on Manu containing no such quotations at all, and very few quotations from Nárada in general, these have not been given.

The many various readings which the quotations contain have *not* been given in the Appendix, except where they have been substituted for the readings of the MSS. Such Çlokas have been marked by an asterisk (*), and the more important alterations of this kind as well as other conspicuous deviations from the text of one MS. or of both MSS. have been stated and justified in the Critical Notes. In general I have retained the readings of the MSS. as far as possible; for though they are many centuries younger than the Dharmanibandhas, the Mitákshará especially, it seems highly probable, on the other hand, that the authors of these latter works quoted mostly from memory. The inaccuracy which this habit must have called forth, accounts for the fact also, that they quote a considerable number of Çlokas as Nárada's, and as Manu's, Yájnavalkyas, etc., which are not found in the texts of these Smṛitis.

The English versions of some Sanskrit Digests, and, among these, especially Colebrooke's excellent translation of the bulky work of Jaganátha, which has stood the test of nearly fourscore years and corresponding progress of Sanskrit scholarship, have furnished a very material aid not only in establishing a correct text, but, of course, also in rendering it in English. Not a few Çlokas in the Law Section of this work have been literally transcribed from the versions contained in Colebrooke's Digest, and, in the Chapter on Inheritance, also from those contained in his translations of the Dáyabhága of Jímútaváhana and of the

Mitákshará. Such deviations from his renderings as were occasioned by different readings, or by slight omissions or those misapprehensions of his, which originate in the peculiar nature of Jagannátha's work —being a mere collection of disconnected Çlokas— have been noticed and explained in foot-notes or in the Appendix; some trifling, and chiefly verbal, alterations excepted. Important deviations from the renderings of other passages of our work, which are contained in Borrodaile's, Tagore's, and Bühler's versions of the Vyavahâramayúkha, Vivádachintámani, and Nárada's Dáyabhága (xiii. Head of Dispute), have likewise been adverted to.

When the printing of this work was nearly completed, I received from Benares, through the kindness of Dr. Thibaut, most unexpectedly, a copy of a third MS. of the Sanskrit text. It is quite recent, but, as far as a somewhat cursory examination has shown, it stands nearer to the original text than both L and B, though it is closely allied to them or to their *codex archetypus*. It is true that there is a gap in the first part of it, ch. ii, 18– iii, 18 having been omitted in consequence of a clerical error. But, on the other hand, it contains several Çlokas in various other places, which, though not found in the other MSS., are evidently genuine, and have in my translation been in part supplied from the quotations of the Digests. It also corroborates a considerable part of the rest of my emendations of the text; so that it would have saved much trouble if it had been received at an earlier time. Even where it contains the same errors, interpolations, etc., as the two other MSS., it is serviceable in confirming on its part the inference, which has been drawn from different reasons above, that there exists no other version of Nárada besides the one here translated.

Of the new results to be derived from this MS., all those which are of importance for the present work have been stated in the Addenda, pp. xxxi–xxxiii.

With the ample materials now brought together I am preparing a critical edition of the text, in which I propose to give all the various readings of the Benares as well as of the London and Berlin MSS.

Of the uncertainties and, perhaps, misapprehensions, some portions of this translation contain (*v.* notes and Appendix) in spite of the laborious and painstaking method which has been throughout followed in preparing it, nobody can be better aware than its author. I beg, however, critics to consider that I have been placed in a more difficult position than, probably, all former translators of a Sanskrit law-book: most of these enjoyed all the well-known privileges of scholars living in India, which are doubly valuable for translations of law-books, on account of their relation to the social customs of a nation; and the rest had at least the help of good printed editions of, and running commentaries on, the Sanskrit texts they translated.

If the present work is well received, it will be followed by a translation of one or two of the mediæval treatises. The want of translations of Sanskrit law-books having been often lamented,* it is hoped that a translation of the most luminous, complete, and sysematic *ancient* treatise on Hindu Law will be welcome, not only to Sanskrit scholars, but to the larger circle of those who take an interest in Indian antiquities, or in comparative jurisprudence, or in the practical aspect of Hindu Law. If such be the case, I trust that it will convey a more correct and more favourable impression of native Hindu legislation than either the code of Manu or Jagannáthá's Digest,† the two most widely-spread works on Hindu Law in general, could give. The reproaches heaped upon the latter work concern but its awkward compiler, but Jones's translation of Manu has called forth the severest censure upon the whole spirit of Hindu legislation. Nor are the charges which Mill in his eloquent "History of India," Duncker in his "Geschichte der Arier," have brought against Manu, without foundation.

But with the Náradasmṛiti the case is different. The Hindu lawyers, it is true, rank Nárada with Manu, and attribute an equal authority to all the ancient legislators, though they refer to the former more often, perhaps, than to any other, so that, for instance, his Chapter on Inheritance contains hardly one Çloka

* See, for instance, Burnell, Preface to Dáyavibhága (Madras, 1868), Goldstücker, On the Deficiencies in the Present Administration of Hindu Law, (London, 1871), p. 3[illegible].

† Its translator, Colebrooke, himself was the first to express a highly unfavourable opinion upon this work, *v.* Preface to "Two Treatises on Inheritance," in Stokes' H. L. B. p. 172.

which is not quoted in one of the Dharmanibandhas. But from an European point of view it may safely be asserted that the Náradasmṛiti occupies a far more distinguished position in the development of Hindu legislation than the code of Manu, perhaps the very highest, as it stands in the middle between the primitive stage of development, which the former represents, and the artificial systems of the later legislators or the learned pedantry of the Commentators. Nothing, certainly, can be more unfounded, with regard to Nárada, than the charge of unsystematic treatment of the law, which Mill has brought against Manu. The judicatory, more especially the law of witnesses, deserves the praise which Sir Th. Strange,* and, reluctantly, even Mill, has bestowed upon this part of the legislation, in a far higher degree than the corresponding rules of Manu. And, though some of the laws may seem strange to us, and though the privileges granted to the Brahmins are certainly repugnant to our sense of equity, the greater part of Nárada's precepts are sensible enough, the draconic legislation on criminal justice excepted, which, however, seems to have been antiquated even long before his time.

But that which is perhaps the highest encomium that can be bestowed upon a Hindu law-book, is deserved by the civil laws of the Náradasmṛiti, in that they are not mere theoretical rules and precepts, but such as have, doubtless, been actually administered.

J. JOLLY.

*Würzburg, December*, 1875.

* Hindu Law, vol. i. (London, 1830), p. 311.

## ABBREVIATIONS USED IN THIS WORK.

*Dáyabh.*—Dáya-Bhága, a Treatise on Inheritance, by Jímúta Váhana, transl. by Colebrooke. Stokes' Hindu Law Books (Madras, 1865), pp. 181–363.

*Dig.* or *Col. Dig.*—A Digest of Hindu Law on Contracts and Successions, by Jagannátha, transl. by Colebrooke, 3rd ed., Madras, 1864.

*Manu.*—Manusaṃhitá, with the Commentary of Kullúka, edited by Çríjívánandavidyáságara. Calcutta, 1874.

*May.*—Vyavahára Mayúkha, transl. by Borrodaile. Stokes' H. L. B. pp. 1–168.

*Mit.*—Mitákshará, Vyavahára Section, edited by Sri Lakshmi Náráyaṇa. Calcutta, 1829.

*Col. Mit.*—The Law of Inheritance, from the Mitákshará. Stokes' H. L. B., pp. 364-467.

*Ragh.*—Vyavahára Tatwa. A Treatise on Judicial Proceedings, by Raghunandana, ed. by Lakshmi Náráyan Sermá. Calcutta, 1828.

*Tagore.*—Viváda Chintámani, transl. by Tagore. Calcutta, 1863.

*Vír.*—Víramitrodaye Vyavahárádhyáyaḥ. Edited by Çríjívánandavidyáságara. Calcutta, 1875.

*Viv.*—Váchaspatimiçra's Vivádachintámani. Calcutta, 1837.

*Yájn.*—Yájnavalkya's Gesetzbuch, von Stenzler. Breslau, 1849.

Besides, in the Appendix, B refers to the Berlin, L to the London MS. of Nárada. In the work itself, those words which are not contained in the Sanskrit text have been *italicized.*

# ADDENDA.

The copy of the Benares MS., Ben, which was not received from India till nearly the whole of the present work had been printed, besides containing some errors of its own (*v.* Pref., p. xxiv), partly partakes of the mistakes contained in B L, partly confirms the corrections, insertions, and omissions I have made in the text of these MSS., and, thirdly, in a very few cases, furnishes better readings than those followed in this translation, or supplies omissions.

1. It shares the false readings, omissions, and interpolations of the two other MSS., which have been noticed in the notes and Appendix: 1, 25. 36. 37. 46. 51. 55. 59. 3, 16. 17. 39. 4, 19. 20. 30. 39. 41. 47. 60. 71. 5, 7. 40. 43. 48. 56. 69. 104. 7, 6. 14. v, 40. vi, 7. 12. viii, 5. ix, 9. x, 6. xi, 6. 27. 33. 36. xii, 10. 31. 77. 82. 86. 89. 105. xiii, 18. 21. 24. 30. 34. 48. xiv, 19. 25. xv, 11. xvi, 7. xvii, 1. 9. 39.

2. It confirms the alterations made, readings preferred, or omissions supplied in this translation: 1, 27. 35. 37. 2, 8b–11. 3, 18, 19. 21. 36. 66. 4, 1. 9. 18. 34. 5, 9. 13. 26. 27. 62–68. 129 (where my translation

differs from Stenzler's Z. d. d. m. G. 668, because he quotes this passage from the Mit. and Vír., which lawbooks exhibit a different reading of it). ii, 5. iii, 4. iv, 3. v, 26. 32. 39. vi, 8. 13. 16. 22. vii, 4. 7. viii, 10. 12. ix, 9. xi, 8. 15. 18. 20. 26. 40. xii, 19. 27. 40. 46–51. 65. 66. 69. 78. 81. 93. 101. xiii, 6. 11. 14. 23. 32. 42. xiv, 7. xv, 5. 26. 30. xvii, 19. 35. In most of these cases the readings, which I have translated, are literally found in Ben; in the other cases—in such cases especially, where hemistichs or Çlokas wanting in B and L have been supplied from elsewhere—they agree with the readings of Ben as to the sense, though not in every single word.

3. 8, 5. Ben has: *vishasya tu palárddhárddhách chhatabhágaṃ ghṛitayutam*, etc., which is evidently the correct reading of this passage. The translation of the first half of this Çloka, p. 52, has to be altered therefore into: "A hundredth part of a half of a half *pala* of the poison, etc.—5, 121. My conjecture in the note to this passage (p. 47, nt. 2) is supported in so far as Ben exhibits a different reading, and inserts a whole Çloka here, which, though wanting in B and L, is apparently genuine. The following words have therefore to be substituted for 121 and for the first sentence in 122 from "an honest man—fasten it:" "The king should have a wooden *beam of the* balance made, by which the scales shall be suspended, four hands long, equitable, and having the required qualities. He shall *also* cause two posts to be erected, upon even ground, directed from south to north, and both in one line, and have the

*beam of the* balance fastened by *the transverse beam which connects* them. *Namely,* an honest man should fasten the *beam of the* balance *upon* the middle *of the transverse beam,* after it has," etc. The contradiction between 120 and 121 is not removed by this alteration. —6, 7. The following Çloka is inserted in Ben and has to be supplied in my translation, p. 49, after "circles" (l. 17.): "He shall not overstep a circle, nor shall he place his foot behind. Having thus passed through the seven circles successively, *and* reached," etc. —After xii, 66 (p. 88), Ben inserts the following Çloka: "The exchange of benefits, dallying with each other, touching of each other's ornaments or clothes, or sitting on the same bed, are all considered as adulterous acts." It is true that the Viváda Chintámani, p. 110, quotes this Çloka as Vyása's, and that it occurs also in Manu 8, 357, but it may be common to the three authors, and it certainly fits very well in this place.

3, 67 also Ben exhibits a reading, which seems preferable to that of B L rendered in this translation, viz., *bráhmaṇasya tv avikreyam* for *bráhmaṇasya cha vikreyam.* The version of this Çloka (p. 22) has to be altered therefore into: "Nor may a *Brahmin* sell," etc., v. Manu 10, 86–89.—The two Çlokas and one hemistich, which Ben inserts in various places (2, 9. xvii, 34. xiv, 8) appear to be spurious.

# CONTENTS.

# INTRODUCTION.

Salutation to the holy *Ganeça.*

1.* Thus he said: The venerable *Manu Prajápati* composed for the benefit of all *human* beings a book founded upon custom and law, which consisted of twenty-four divisions, *in which as many subjects were contained, viz.*, first, the creation of the world, a classification of the beings *in it*, an enumeration of the countries assigned to them, the characteristics of a judicial assembly, *the right seasons* for the reading of the Vedas and of the Vedángas and *the rules* for offerings, customary law, judicature, the extirpation of evil-doers, the conduct prescribed for kings, the duties of the *four* classes, and the classification of the *four* orders, marriage laws, the relations between man and wife, the order of heirs *entitled to succession*, the offering of *çraddhás*, rules of purification, a list of legitimate and of prohibited eatables, a declaration of

* The division of this introductory chapter into paragraphs *is not* according to the MSS., which differ in this respect, and follow both of them a highly arbitrary mode of division.

articles which may or may not be sold, with a classification of offences, a description of Heaven and Hell, and *an enumeration of* penances, the *Upanishads,* and the mysteries. It contained a hundred thousand Çlokas.

2. *Prajápati* having composed this book, which was arranged in a thousand chapters, delivered it to the divine sage *Nárada.* He then read it and thought by himself: "This book cannot be easily studied by human beings on account of its length." Therefore he abridged it in twelve thousand Çlokas and delivered it to *Sumati,* the son of *Bṛhigu.*

3. He too read it and bethought himself, what human capacity had been brought to through the *successive* lessening of life; wherefore he reduced it to four thousand.

4. It is this *second* abridgement by *Sumati* which mortals read, whilst the gods, *Gandharvas,* and so on, read the original code consisting of a hundred thousand Çlokas, which begins with the following Çloka: "This universe was involved in darkness and could nowhere be discovered; then the holy, self-existing spirit appeared with his four faces."*

5. From this beginning chapter follows chapter in regular succession. There the ninth chapter is headed: "On Judicial Procedure." Of this chapter *Nárada,* the divine sage, made the following general abstract in form of short rules (*sútras*).† It begins thus:—

* This verse corresponds with the 5th and 6th Çlokas of *our* Manu, or properly speaking, with the first and second, as the four opening Çlokas of this work are apparently a later addition.

† *imám . . . sútrastháníyáṃ mátṛikáṃ chakára.* The meaning assigned to *mátṛiká* in the above translation is not given in Böthlingk-Roth's Dictionary, s. v.; but this word certainly means

"summary or general part" in the Mit. 139, where the introductory section of the chapter on ordeals is concluded by the words: *iti divya-mátṛiká.* The similar meaning of "extract or epitome" is not seldom expressed by *sútra*, which word also occurs in our passage. Sir W. Jones in his (very free) translation of part of this introduction (Preface to Manu, p. xix.) has "Nárada's abridgement." Our work, or the first part of it, is again termed a *mátṛiká*, more especially a vyavahára mátṛiká, *i.e.*, a summary of proceedings at law, in the phrase inserted at the close of ch. i.: iti çrínáradíye dharmaçástre vyavahāramátrikáyám prathamo' dhyáyah.

## [PART I.—JUDICATURE.]

### I. Chapter.

1. Judicial procedure has been instituted for the protection of the human race, as a safeguard of law, and in order to take off from kings the responsibility for crimes committed in their kingdoms.

2. When humanity was strictly virtuous and veracious, there existed no quarrels, nor hatred, nor selfishness.

3. Virtue having become extinct among men, judicial procedure has been established; and the king having the privilege of inflicting punishments, has been instituted judge of law-suits.

4. Written proof and witnesses are the two expedients to be resorted to for ascertaining disputed facts *in a contest* between two litigants.

5. Law-suits are of two kinds, attended by wager, or not attended by wager; attended by wager are those, when it is promised in a written declaration to discharge a certain sum over and above the fine *in case of defeat.*

6. In a law-suit attended by wager, the loser has to pay the wager made by himself, and a fine, to the king.

7. But the declaration is pronounced to be the essence of a judicial proceeding; if he gets the worst

of it, the claimant loses his cause; if he gets the better of it, he wins it.

8. Family-councils, companies *of artisans,* assemblies *of cohabitants,* an appointed *judge,* and the king *himself* are resorts for the trial of law-suits; and among these, the last in order is superior to the preceding.

9. Judicial proceedings have four feet, and four courses; they benefit four, regard four, and produce four results.

10. Their constituent parts are eight in number, the heads of dispute eighteen with hundred ramifications, their causes three, the modes of complaint two, *as also* two sides and two eventualities.

11. The law, the issue of the case, the conduct *of the parties,* and an edict from the king: these are the four feet of a judicial proceeding; each following is weightier than the preceding.

12. Law is based upon truth; the issue of the case *depends upon the deposition of* the witnesses; the conduct *of the parties* becomes manifest at the trial; the *king's* edict depends upon the king's pleasure.

13. A judicial proceeding is said to have four courses, because it takes a different course, according as the different expedients of conciliation etc.* are adopted. It is said to benefit four, because it protects the four orders.

14. It is said to regard four, because the perpetrator of the deed, the witnesses, the judges, and the king are equally concerned by it. (Cf. ch. ii. 18).

* The three remaining expedients are, according to Manu, 7, 107, and Kullúka's gloss, "presents, division, and force."

15. Because it promotes justice, gain, glory, renown, therefore it is said to produce four results.

16. The eight constituent parts *of a judicial proceeding* are the king, his officer, the assessors, the law-book, the accountant, and scribe, gold and fire *for ordeals,* and water *for refreshment.*

17. Recovery of a Debt, Deposits, Concerns among Partners, Abstraction of Gift, Breach of promised Obedience,

18. Non-payment of Wages, Sale without Ownership, Non-delivery of a commodity sold, Rescission of Purchase,

19. Breach of Order, Contests about Boundaries, the Duties of Man and Wife, the Law of Inheritance, Violence,

20. Abuse and Assault, Gambling, and Miscellaneous Disputes; these are the eighteen heads of dispute.

21. Of these again there are one hundred and eight subdivisions; therefore a judicial proceeding is said to have a hundred ramifications, owing to the diversity of men's claims.

22. Because it is instituted from one of these three causes: love, anger, and cupidity, therefore it is said to have three causes; these are the three motives for going to law.

23. It is said to have two kinds of claims, because they rest either on suspicion or on facts; on suspicion, if the defendant has frequented bad society; on facts, if the stolen goods are produced.

24. Because it concerns two parties, it is said to have two sides; of these the charge is called claim, the rejoinder answer.

25. Because both true and false statements are made in course of a judicial proceeding, it is said to have two courses; a true statement is one agreeing with the facts, a false one is a wrong one.

26. A dutiful king shall check falsehood, where it has not been checked *by others*, and strive after truth, since it is justice that happiness springs from.

27. As seven flames rise from a fire, so do seven rewards wait upon a good king, who passes just decisions in law-suits.

28. Virtue, gain, good report, worldly fame, conquests, the esteem of his subjects, and an eternal residence in heaven *will wait upon him*.

29. Therefore a king having seated himself on the throne of judgment, should discard interested motives, and deal even-handed justice to all his subjects, as if he were *Vaivasvata* himself.

30. He should carefully examine all claims, one after the other, according to the respective rank of the claimants, considering what would be useful or injurious, and just or unjust,

31. Taking the law-code * for his guide, and abiding by the opinion pronounced by the chief judge.

32. Firstly, the litigants have to appear *before the court*, secondly the drift of their dispute *has to be expounded, then comes* the examination, *and lastly* the

* Colebrooke O. H. C. etc. Ess. i, 511, "placing the sacred code of law before him."—Here, then, the well-known statement of Strabo, or his informants, that in the Indian courts of justice no written codes used to be consulted, is refuted. Compare also above Çl. 16, where the law-book is mentioned as one of the constituent parts of a judicjal proceeding.

sentence; thus the trial of a law-suit consists of four parts.

33. The trial should be conducted discreetly and skilfully, and without neglecting either sacred or profane rules of conduct.

34. Where religious and secular rules are at variance, the secular rules have to be put aside and the religious precepts to be followed.

35. The law ordains to take logic for one's guide, when the sacred law cannot be applied, for *the evidence in* a law-suit *is more* decisive *than the law,* and overrules the law.

36. Holy Law is of a subtle nature and has to be treated with great care. An honest man may become a thief, and a thief an honest man.

37. Cases decided by women, at night, abroad, in the inside of a house, and by enemies, shall be reversed.

38. Let *the judge* proceed slowly *in all trials relating to* debt and so on, on account of the intricacy of law-cases and the insufficiency of memory.

39. If the defendant does not speak, he must be confined and punished according to law, and if he does not refute the statement of his adversary, he has to pay the money, which he is sued for.

40. A charge relating to a cow, land, gold, a woman, theft, the two kinds of insult, and violence, has to be answered immediately.

41. One may wait for one day, for five, or three days, or three half-months, or seven days, if the claim relates to a debt or the like.

42. He who tries to enforce a claim, without giving notice to the king *previously,* shall receive a severe punishment, and his claim shall be rejected.

43. A claimant may arrest his adversary until the arrival of the summons, if the latter *tries to* evade the claim he is about to prefer, or does not refute his charge.

44. Arrest is four-fold: local, temporary, inhibition from travelling, and from pursuing one's occupation; and the person under arrest is not allowed to break it.

45. No culpability attaches to him who breaks an arrest put upon him while crossing a river or while passing a forest, in an inhospitable country, or, *generally speaking*, in perilous circumstances.

46. One, who having been arrested at a proper time, breaks his arrest, is to be fined; and one arresting improperly is liable to penalty.

47. One desirous of celebrating his nuptials, afflicted with an illness, about to perform a sacrifice, distressed, sued by another party, employed in the king's service,

48. Cowherds while tending their cattle, husbandmen in the act of cultivation, artisans engaged in their trades, soldiers engaged in warfare,

49. A minor, a messenger, one about to give alms or fulfilling a vow, and one surrounded by difficulties, must not be arrested *by the adversary* nor summoned by the king.

50. A person arraigned, not having refuted the adversary's charge, cannot bring forward any claim, nor is it allowed to injure one accused by another party by trying to intimidate him (?) *

51. No one must alter the charge he has brought *before the judge*; he who rests his claim on different

* *na.. chihnakṛid beddhum arhati.* Cf. Böthlingk-Roth, s.v. *chihnakárin.*

grounds from those first adduced by him, loses his cause.

52. Nor must one bring forward a false claim; *for* it is a sin unjustly to accuse a man; the punishment inflicted in such law-suits falls upon the claimant.

53. A man may delay his answer, as long as the law permits it; if he does not speak in the judicial assembly, or alters his former statements, it shows that he is in the wrong.

54. He who does not obey the summons or, having appeared before the court, does not answer the charge, is to be fined by the king as having lost his cause.

55. After the sentence has been passed, evidence is to no purpose, unless it consist in *the deposition of* witnesses, or in documents, referred to in a former stage *of the trial.*

56. As the powers of rain are lavished upon ripe grain, so evidence is no longer useful, if once the decision has been passed.

57. Even false statements are examined if made in proper time; but what is left unsaid through inadvertency has no effect, even though it be true.

58. He who thinks a law case to have been wrongly decided and judged, may have it tried anew, if he pays the double amount of the fine inflicted.

59. If an unjust sentence has been passed, the judges have to pay that fine; for nobody certainly commits an offence without being liable to punishment for it.

60. Whether it be through passion, ignorance, or avarice, that a judge pronounces an unfair opinion, he must be considered as no assessor of the court, and the king should severely punish that sinful man.

61. But a king, especially, who is careful to discharge

his duty, must endeavour to distinguish right from wrong, because human minds are subtle.

62. There are men who bear false testimony from avarice; and there are other wicked men who forge written documents.

63. Therefore both documents and witnesses have to be carefully examined by the king, the former by *inquiring into* the condition of the writing, the latter *by inquiring* into the nature of their deposition.

64. There are skilful men who imitate the handwriting of others; therefore similarity of handwriting affords no conclusive proof.

65. Liars may have the bearing of veracious men, and veracious men look like liars. *Men in general* appear in various shapes; thus caution is required.

66. The sky seems to be a roof, and the fire-fly * appears to be a fire; yet there is no roof to the atmosphere, nor fire in the fire-fly.

67. Hence it is right to examine a fact strictly, even though it occurred in the inquirer's own sight. He who ascertains facts by rigid investigation, does not deviate from justice.

68. A king thus constantly paying attention to the trial of law-suits, here acquires brilliant glory, and hereafter reaches the abode of the sun.

* *Khadyota*, which has been taken above in the common acceptation of the term, Colebrooke translates: "The luminary which shines in the heavens," *i.e.* the sun. But the well-known phenomenon of the Indian fire-fly, whose intense brilliancy has often been described by travellers, might well suggest the above simile to an author.

## II. Chapter.

### *On Courts of Justice.*

1. One who is not appointed *to be a member of the court* must on no account speak at the trial of a law-suit; but by him, who has been appointed, an impartial opinion ought to be given.

2. Whether appointed or not appointed, one who is conversant with the law has a right to speak; for he whose conduct is regulated by the law, delivers a speech inspired by the deity.

3. For the trial of all law-suits persons familiar with many branches of science should be appointed; no prudent man would entrust *this task* to a single person, though a virtuous one.

4. Whatever judgement ten men versed in the Veda and jurisprudence, or three men familiar with the Veda, pass upon the case in hand is right, and a valid sentence.

5. The king *alone*, being the supreme ruler, is entitled to decide knotty law-cases; therefore a *private* man should not pass a sentence alone; his opinion would leave room for doubt.

6. A judge, pronouncing a fair sentence, incurs neither enmity nor sin; but one who speaks differently incurs both.

7. The king should appoint, as members of the court, honest men of tried integrity, who are able to support

the burden of the administration of justice like bulls *bearing a heavy load.*

8. The assessors of the king's courts of judicature should be men skilled in matters of law, sprung from good families, veracious, and impartial towards friend and foe.

9. Divine justice is *represented* as a bull, and the gods consider him who impedes justice as a *Vṛishala,* or one who slays a bull. Let no man therefore violate justice.

10. The only firm friend who follows you, even after death, is justice; everything else is extinct with the body.

11. When law-suits are justly decided, the judges obtain their own absolution. Their innocence depends on the justice *of their decisions;* therefore should equitable judgements only be pronounced.

12. Justice, wounded by the arrows of falsehood, roars in the midst of the assembly, as she is exposed to the fatal attacks of wicked men, who prefer iniquity *to justice.**

13. Where justice is slain by iniquity, and truth by falsehood, the judges, who look on *without giving redress,* shall also be slain.

14. Justice being destroyed, will destroy; being preserved, will preserve; therefore it must never be violated, lest, being violated, it should destroy *thyself and* us.

15. When justice, wounded by iniquity, approaches,

* Colebrooke, Ess. i. 523. "Justice, wounded by the shafts of falsehood, roars in the midst of the assembly against injustice set before him: this evil being should be slain, EVEN BY THE WICKED."

enters the court, and the judges extract not the dart, they also *will be* wounded *by it.*

16. Either the court must not be entered, or law and truth must be openly declared; but that man is criminal who either says nothing, or speaks falsely.

17. But judges who, after having repaired to the court, sit there in silent meditation, and do not deliver a candid opinion, as they ought, are all guilty of *deliberate* falsehood.

18. One quarter of the iniquity committed falls upon the party in a cause, one quarter on his witnesses, one quarter upon all the assessors of the court, and one quarter on the king.

19. Therefore should a judge, when he has entered the court, divest himself from both love and hatred, and deliver a fair opinion, in order that he may not go to hell.

20. The king is blameless, the judges are absolved *from iniquity,* the sin falls upon the sinner*'s head alone,* when those who deserve punishment receive it.

21. As a blind man, heedless, swallows fish with the bones,* *so does he* who enters a court of justice, and there pronounces a perverse opinion, from mistake of facts.

22. As a skilful† surgeon extracts a dart by cautious efforts, so should the chief judge extract the darts *of iniquity* from the law-suit.

23. When all the members of a judicial assembly opine, "this is right," the court is relieved from the

* Colebrooke, On Hindu Courts etc., l. c. 522: "thorny fish."

† This word is wanting in Colebrooke's translation of this Çloka, l. c. 523.

dart *of iniquity;* but the dart remains *in the wound,* if they do not say so.

24. That is not a judicial assembly where the elders are missing, nor are they elders who do not pronounce a just opinion, nor is that a just opinion which is against equity, nor is that equitable which is contaminated with fraud.

---

## III. Chapter.

### *Recovery of a Debt.*

1. What may or may not be lent, by whom, to whom, and in what form, with the rules for delivery and receipt, are comprised in law under the *title of* Recovery of a Debt.

2. After the death of their father the sons shall pay his debt according to their respective shares, if they separate; or else, if they do not separate, that son who takes the burden *of a paterfamilias* on himself, shall pay it.

3. A debt contracted by an uncle, a brother, or mother, who do not live separately, for the benefit of the family, shall be paid by all the joint-proprietors.

4. The grandsons shall pay the debt of their grandfather, which having been legitimately inherited by the sons, has not been paid by them; *the obligation* ceases with the fourth descendant.

5. Fathers desire offspring for their own sake, reflecting, "this son will redeem me from every debt whatsoever due to superior and inferior beings."

6. Therefore a son begotten by him should relinquish his own property, and assiduously redeem his father from debt, lest he fall to a region of torment.

7. He who has received more than his due and does not give it *back* to the owner, is born again in his house as his slave, servant, wife, or cattle.

8. If a man does not repay what has been borrowed for use, or a debt, or what he has promised, that sum may be increased even to a milliard.

9. The milliard being completed he [the debtor] is born again as a slave in his [the creditor's] house in each successive birth, till the debt is paid.*

10. When a devotee, or a man who maintained a sacrificial fire, dies without having discharged his debt, the whole merit of his devotions, or of his perpetual fire, belongs to his creditor.

11. The father shall not pay his son's debts, but the son those of his father, those excepted, which have been contracted from love, anger, drunkenness, in gambling, and in bailing.

12. A father shall pay such debts of his son as have been contracted by his order, or for the maintenance of the family, or in order to pay a fine.

13. The householder is liable for whatever has been spent for the benefit of the family by the pupil, apprentice, slave, wife, agent, or commissioned servant.

14. When the father, uncle, or elder brother, is gone abroad, the son, *or nephew, or younger brother* need not pay his debt, until twenty years have elapsed.

15. The debts of sick, mad, superannuated, and long

* Borrodaile, in a version of 8 and 9, May. V. 4, 11, appears to have had a different reading before him.

absent persons, such debts shall be paid by the son, even while they are alive.

16. Any parcener may be compelled to pay another's *share of* a debt contracted by joint-tenants, while they were *all* alive; but, if they be dead, the son of one is not liable to pay the debt of another.

17. A woman is not bound to pay the debts of her husband or son, unless she have promised to do so, or contracted them jointly with them.

18. The debts contracted by the husband * shall be discharged by the widow, if sonless, or if her husband has enjoined her to do so on his death-bed, or if she inherits the estate; for whosoever takes the estate, must pay the debts, *with which it is encumbered.*

19. Debts contracted by the wife never fall upon the husband, unless they were contracted *for necessaries* at a time of distress; for the household expenses have to be defrayed by the man.

20. If a woman who has male issue desert her son, and recur to another man, her son must pay the whole debt, if she has no property of her own.

21. But if a woman goes to live with another man, carrying her riches and offspring, he must pay the debts of her husband, or part with her.

22. He who takes possession of a *man's* wife, daughter-in-law, or grandson's wife, and of the assets of his wife, is liable for the debts, as well as he who takes possession of the estate.

23. In all the *four* classes, one after the other, wives

* Colebrooke, Dig. i, 5, ccxiii, where this Çloka is quoted: "the debt of her *sister* enjoining payment." He must have had a different, and a worse, reading before him.

and goods go together; he who takes a man's wives, takes his property too.

24. He who takes the wife of a poor and sonless dead man, becomes liable for his debts; for the wife is considered as the *dead* man's property.

25. Of the successor to the estate, the guardian of the widow, and the son, he who takes the assets, becomes liable for the debts; the son, if there be no guardian of the widow, nor successor to the estate; and the person who took the widow, if there be no successor to the estate, nor son.

26. He who takes possession of the last of the *svairiṇís* and of the first of the *punarbhús*,* is liable for the debts contracted by the husband.

27. Women's business transactions are null and void, except in case of distress, especially the gift, pawning, or sale, of a house or field.

28. Women are not entitled to make a gift or sale; a woman can only take a life-interest, whilst she is living together with the rest of the family.

29. Such *transactions of women* are valid, when the husband has given his consent, or, in default of the husband, the son, or, in default of husband and son, the king.

30. She may enjoy or give away goods according to her pleasure, except immoveables; for she has no proprietary rights over fields and the like.

31. The transaction of a slave has no validity either, except if he had the authority of his master for it: a slave is not his own master.

32. If a son has made a transaction without his

* For an enumeration of the *svairiṇís* (disloyal wives) and *punarbhús* (twice-married wcmen), see below 12, 46 foll.

father's consent, it is likewise declared to be invalid: a slave and a son are both alike *in this respect at least.*

33. A minor also, though he be independent, is not liable for debts; *true* independence rests with the senior, *the right of* seniority *again* is based on virtue and strength.

34. Three persons are independent in this world, a teacher, a king, and, in every class throughout the whole system of classes, he who is the head of his family.

35. All the subjects are dependent, the sovereign is independent; the pupil is held to be dependent, but the teacher enjoys independence.

36. Women, sons, slaves and attendants are dependent; but the head of a family is subject to no control in disposing of his hereditary property.

37. A child is comparable to an embryo up to his eighth year; a boy is called *pauganda* (youth) up to his sixteenth year.

38. Afterwards he is of age and independent, in case his parents be dead; during their life-time he is dependent even though he be grown old.

39. Of the two parents the father has the greater authority, since the seed is worth more *than the field;* in default of the father the mother, in her default the first-born.

40. These are never subject to any control from dependent persons; they are fully entitled to give orders and make gifts or sales.

41. A transaction made by a child or a minor is declared by those learned in the law to have no validity before the law.

42. A transaction also of an independent man, but

who has lost the control over his actions (*prakṛiti*), is declared to be null and void, because he has lost his independence.

43. Persons acting from love or anger, the distressed, and those who are beset by dangers or calamities, or biassed by friendship or hatred, are declared to have lost the control over their actions.

44. The oldest or the most able member of a family, and *in general every* one who has not lost the control over his actions, these are able to perform valid transactions; what a dependent person does, is invalid.

45. Work of all kinds is productive of wealth, exertion is required for the acquisition of it, preservation and augmentation in using it: these are the rules regarding wealth.

46. Again, it is declared to be of three sorts, pure, spotted, and black, each kind being in its turn divided into seven species.

47. What is *acquired* by *teaching* the Vedas, by courage, or devotion; *what is received* with a damsel, from a pupil, or for a sacrifice; and *what* is obtained by inheritance, such is the seven-fold *distinction of* pure property.

48. What is gained by usury, agriculture, and traffick, or *received* as tolls, as wages for artistic performances, or *as a return* for a service rendered or benefit conferred, is considered as spotted* wealth.

49. What is acquired by servile attendance, by gambling, by robbery, by *inflicting* pain, by disguise,

* Colebrooke, Dig. ii. 4, xxvii. takes the term *cavala* metaphorically: "partaking of the quality of passion," and mentions six species only of this kind of wealth.

by larceny, and by fraud, is considered as black wealth.

50. Hence it is that purchase and sale, giving and taking, and various other transactions, as well as enjoyment, arise.

51. The reward which a man gets in this world and hereafter, will be in strict accordance with what kind of things he has had to do with.

52. *Wealth* is of twelve sorts again according to the class to which you belong; *among these,* three are common *to all classes,* there are nine others *confined to a special class.*

53. What has been inherited, friendly gifts, and the dower of a wife; these are the three kinds of wealth common to all classes indiscriminately.

54. The descriptions of property peculiar to the class of *Brahmins* are three, viz., what has been obtained as alms, by sacrificing, and from a pupil.

55. The special property of a *Kshatriya* is likewise threefold, viz., what has been gained in warfare, by work, and in the shape of fines in law-suits.

56. The *Vaiçyas* too have three kinds of property of their own, viz., *what has been acquired* by tilling, the tending of cows, and trading; the *Çúdras* live by the presents they receive from them [*i.e.,* from the three higher classes].

57. These are the legitimate modes of acquisition for all classes; all others are illegitimate, except in cases of overwhelming distress.

58. In cases of distress a *Brahmin* may adopt the mode of living *of the class* next to him in rank, and even the mode of living of a *Vaiçya* is by no means dishonourable to him *in such cases.*

59. *But* a Brahmin shall never perform vile work, nor a vile man the work of a Brahmin; for both *offences* entail loss of caste.

61. No work is permitted to them, which is either far above or far below their rank; but it is well if they take to occupations of a middle sort, which are common to all classes.

62. As soon as a *Brahmin* has got over his difficulties by means of the wealth acquired by living like a *Kshatriya*, let him do penance and give up living like a *Kshatriya*.

63. He who foolishly persists in this way of living, having taken pleasure in it, is proclaimed to be a *Káṇḍapṛishṭha*, and ejected from his caste for having swerved from the path of duty.

64. While gaining his substance like a *Vaiçya* a *Brahmin* must never sell milk, sour milk, butter, honey, bees-wax, lac [red dye], alkali, sweets, spirits,

65. Meat, boiled rice, sesam, linen, soma, flowers, fruits, refined sugar, human excrements, weapons, water, salt, cakes, plants, clothes,

66. Silk, leather, bones, leathern oil-bottles, animals whose foot is not cloven, earthenware, buttermilk, hair, saffron, vegetables, and herbs.

67. A *Brahmin* may sell dry wood, grass, fragrant substances, ewe, reeds, mulberry, roots except *Kuça*-grass.

68. Baskets *made of bamboos* split by himself, of fruits the fruit of the *jujube* tree and of the *ainguda* plant, ropes, thread made of cotton, if it be not spoiled.

69. In cases of distress or if it is for a medicine

or for an offering, and if he acts under compulsion, he may sell sesam, grain, and the like.

70. But a *Brahmin* who deviates from the path *of duty* by selling articles which ought not to be sold *by him,* must be brought back to his duty by the king by severe chastisement.

---

## IV. Chapter.

### *On Evidence by Writing.*

1. Those conversant with the rules of evidence * must pay a strict regard to the evidence; evidence loses its force, when it has not its due form.

2. Written proof, witnesses, and possession, these are the three kinds of evidence, on which the right of property rests, *and by means of which* a creditor may recover his loan.

3. A document remains always evidence, witnesses as long as they live, and possession *becomes evidence* after a lapse of time; thus it is propounded in the law-books.

4. What a man is not possessed of, that is not his own, even though there be written proof, and even though witnesses be living; this is especially the case with immoveables.

5. If a man foolishly suffers his property to be enjoyed by strangers, it will become *those strangers'*

* *i.e.*, "the judges," according to the Smṛitichandriká ad h. l., quoted Vír. 105, whose comments I have followed in translating this Çloka.

own through the effect of possession, although the proprietor is known to be alive.

6. Whatever property a proprietor sees with his own eyes being enjoyed by strangers, without for ten years asserting his rights, may not be recovered by him.

7. Because he has been indulgent and looking on without asserting his rights, therefore he will be non-suited, *if* [cf. Çl. 3] *he prefers a claim* after the expiration of the above-mentioned period.

8. If he is neither an idiot nor a *mere* child, and if the chattel is being enjoyed *by a stranger* while he is near, his property in it is extinct by law, and the adverse possessor shall keep it.

9. Pledges, boundaries, the property of children, common deposits, sealed deposits, women, and goods belonging to the king or learned Brahmins are not lost *to the owner* through their being possessed by a stranger.

10. Even pledges etc., are lost, if strangers have enjoyed them for twenty years before the owner's eyes; the property of women and of kings is excepted *from this rule.*

11. The property of women and of kings can never be lost, even though it be enjoyed for hundreds of years *by strangers* who have no title to it.

12. Where possession exists, but no title whatever exists, there a title, but not possession *alone*, can confer *proprietary rights.*

13. A title having been substantiated, the possession becomes valid; it remains invalid *without a proved title.*

14. He who simply declares himself possessed *of a commodity* without having a title *to it*, is to be considered as a thief, in consequence of his pleading such illegitimate possession.

16. He who enjoys without a title for ever so many years, the king of the land should inflict on that sinner the punishment of a thief.

17. What a man possesses without a title, he must not alienate, being *only* the possessor of it; but after the death of the possessor such possessions devolve upon his family.

18. In cases falling within the memory of man* possession of land with a title makes evidence. In cases extending beyond the memory of man, the hereditary succession of three ancestors *is admitted as evidence,* though the title be not produced.

19. If a man is accused by him whom he has injured *by taking possession of his property,*† he cannot escape defeat; only what has formerly been possessed by his fathers, and inherited by him in order, is his legitimate property.

20. When possession has been held, even unlawfully, by three ancestors, including the father *of the present occupant,* that cannot be taken away from him, as having gone in order *through three lives.*

21. Common deposits, stolen goods, unspecified deposits, deposits for whose delivery a certain period has been fixed (?), and what is being possessed in secret, are six things possessed without a title.

22. If a litigant dies while a law-suit *about possessions of his* is pending, the son has to prove his title, *the fact of* his possession being insufficient to decide the suit.

23. What has been in the hands of three ancestors

* *Smárte Kále,* which is fixed at 100 years by the Mitákshará.

† See Appendix.

for a very long time, though they had no title, cannot be lost, having gone in order through three lives.*

24. After the death of a creditor even witnesses are no longer of avail, except if a statement made by the creditor himself on his death-bed *has been preserved.*

25. For after the death of an adversary the deposition of his witnesses loses its force, an attested document only being capable of influencing the sentence in this case.

26. But if a man not unsound in mind has preferred a legitimate claim, a witness may give evidence even after *the claimant's* death, in case it be in a matter touching the six cases of deposit and the rest.†

27. In all business transactions the latest act shall prevail, but in the case of a gift, a pledge, or a purchase, the prior act has the greater force.

28. A contract of delivery and receipt may be made with a view to gain *by the lender* on the principal sum while remaining *with* the debtor; it is called a loan on interest, and money-lenders acquire their substance by it.

29. Interest on loans is of four kinds, according to the law-books: interest paid on an undiminished principal (*káyiká*), periodical interest (*káliká*), stipu-

* This Çloka is a mere repetition of the 20th Çloka; yet it must be genuine, because both Çlokas are quoted as Nárada's in *the same* work (the Víramitrodaya, see Appendix).

† See 21. Macnaghten in his translation of part of the Mitákshará, where this Cloka is quoted (Principles and Precedents of Hindu Law, Madras, 1865, p. 244), refers the words of the text: *shatsu chánváhitádishu* to the "six species of bailments." But Nárada's enumeration of the latter begins with the *nikshepa*, not with the *anváhita* bailment; see iii. head of dispute, 7.

lated interest (*káritá*), and compound interest (*chakravṛiddhi*).

30. Interest at the rate of one *paṇa* or half of a *paṇa*, paid always,* without diminishing the principal (*káyá*) is termed *káyiká*;† that which runs by the month, is named kálika (from *kála* " time expired.")

31. That interest is termed *káritá* or stipulated, which has been promised by the debtor himself. Interest upon interest is named *chakravṛiddhi* (wheel-interest).

32. This is the universal rule for interest to be paid on debts, which, however, may vary according to the *peculiar* usages of the place where the lender is living.

33. Gold, clothes, and grain yield interest twice, thrice, and four times *the principal.* Fluids yield interest eight times the principal, the offspring of women and cattle *constitutes the interest thereof.*

34. Of thread, cotton, substances from which wine or spirits are extracted, lead, tin, weapons of every description, leather, copper, iron, and all other such articles, bricks too, the interest is unlimited (*akshayá*), as has been said by *Manu Prajápati.*

35. Oil of every kind, spirits, honey, and butter, as well as sugar and salt, shall yield interest eight times *the principal.*

36. Loans made from friendship do not yield any interest, unless there be a *special* agreement for it.

* *i.e.* daily, Viv. Chint.

† Yájnavalkya, Vṛihaspati, Vyása on the contrary define káyiká as the interest which accrues from the body of a pledged quadruped, taking *kaya* in its literal sense of " body." See Colebrooke Dig. i, 2, xxxv. and foll.; Víramitr. 294.

But, even without it, interest accrues from such loans after the lapse of six months.

37. This is the interest prescribed for loans made from friendship. But the *rate of* interest, which has been mentioned, is considered as usury upon grain.

38. A *Vaiçya,* however, may get over a time of distress by practising usury, if he likes. A *Brahmin* must not practice usury, even though he be in the extremity of distress.

39. If a debt is to be paid to a *dead Brahmin* creditor who has issue, *it must be paid to them;* if there is no issue, *the king* shall cause the debt to be paid to his kinsmen; on their default, to his distant relatives.

40. And if there are no kinsmen nor persons connected *by sacred studies,* nor distant relatives, it shall be paid to *other* persons of the creditor's class; if none such are present, let him cast it into the waters.

41. A creditor should on receiving his principal give a receipt for it; if he does not give it, although he has been asked for it, he shall lose the rest of his due.

42. On payment of the debt he shall give back the bond, on default of such he shall make a public acknowledgement: thus the creditor and debtor will be mutually acquitted.

43. If the creditor does not receipt the payment of his due or if he does not acknowledge it in public, it *continues to* yield interest to the creditor, because of its not being receipted.

44. There are two ways for affording a guarantee to a creditor, viz., by means of a surety and of a

pledge; a writing and attestation are the two kinds of evidence carrying conviction.

45. Three sorts of sureties, for three purposes, are mentioned by the wise: for appearance, for payment, and for honesty.

46. If a deposit or bail or the rest of a debt is not delivered on demand, *the king* shall cause interest to be paid for it.

47. If the debtors fail in their engagements, or if the creditor's confidence was misplaced, the surety *for payment and for honesty* must pay the debt; and *so must the surety for appearance,* if he do not produce *the debtor.*

48. If a surety for appearance or a surety for honesty should die, their sons are not liable for the debt; but the sons of sureties for payment must pay it.

49. When there are many sureties *jointly bound,* they shall pay *their proportionate shares of* the debt according to contract: when they are bound severally,* the payment shall be made *by any of them,* as the creditor pleases.

50. If the surety, being harrassed by the creditor, discharge the debt, the debtor shall pay twice as much as the surety.

51. That to which a *secondary* title is given (*adhikriyate*) is a pledge (*ádhi*); it is of two sorts: a pledge that is to be released within a specified time, and a pledge that is to be retained as long as the debt is not liquidated.

52. It is again declared to be of two sorts, for

* Yájnavalkya, in the analogous passage ii, 55 of his Law Book has: "if they have all stepped upon the shadow of one man."

custody only and for use. Even so must it be diligently kept; otherwise the pledgee forfeits interest.

53. If the pledge be disfigured through the negligence of the pledgee, the consequence is the same. If *a pledge* be lost, the principal shall be forfeited, unless the loss was caused by Fate or the king.

54. If a pledge, though carefully kept, loses its value in course of time, a second pledge must be given or the debt liquidated.

55. What is given by force, what is by force enjoyed, by force caused to be written, and all other things done by force, Manu has pronounced void.

56. If a rich debtor, through dishonest perverseness, do not pay his debt, *the king* shall force him to pay it * and take five in the hundred of the sum himself.

57. Should a debtor be disabled, by *famine or other* calamity of the time, *from paying the debt*, he shall be only compelled to pay it gradually, according to his means, as he happens to gain property.

58. If the creditor's claim ceases to be admissible through length of time, he may still substantiate it by means of a document, if his tribe acknowledge his claim, or if he has a pledge, or can prove occupancy *of the land in question*.†

59. Written proof is declared to be of two sorts,

* The clause regarding the payment of the debt is wanting in Colebrooke's Digest i, 6, cclxxiv, where this Çloka is quoted.

† With a different division of words: *Játisañjñá-'dhivásánám ágamo lekhyataḥ smṛitah,* instead of *játisañjñá-'dhi-vásánám,* etc., the second hemistich of this difficult Çloka would specify two modes only of substantiating a claim, the first and the third in the above enumeration.

*the first,* in the handwriting of the party himself, *the second,* in that of another person, *the former being valid* without subscribing witnesses, *the latter requiring to be* attested: the validity of both depends on the usage established in the country.

60. That instrument which is not adverse to peculiar local usages, which declares the nature of the pledge made, and which is consistent in import and language, is termed proof.

61. That instrument is not termed proof, which is executed by a person intoxicated, by one under duress, by a female, by a child, and that which is effected by force, by intimidation, and by fraud.

62. A written contract loses its validity in that case also, if the witnesses, creditor, debtor, and writer be dead, unless its validity be insured by means of a pledge.

63. If anything has been received or a *public* announcement been made, a contract retains its validity even after the death of the witnesses.

64. Pledges are declared to be of two sorts, moveable and immoveable; both are valid when there is actual enjoyment, and not otherwise.

65. An instrument which has been produced in due season, proclaimed in public, and *repeatedly* called into remembrance, remains always evidence, even after the death of the witnesses.

66. An instrument, whose purport nobody has heard of, which has remained unknown, or become the object of a law-suit, has no validity, not even while the witnesses are living.

67. In the case of an instrument being deposited in another country, or burnt, or badly written, or

stolen, time must be allowed, if it be in existence; if it be not in existence, the evidence of those who have seen it must be resorted to.

68. If there exist doubts about a document, whether it be genuine or no, its authenticity must be proved by the handwriting of *the party* himself, *by evidence of* the contract, *which it records*, by *peculiar* marks, and by reasonable inference.

69. If a document bears the name of a stranger and is designed for a different purpose, its authenticity has to be established with especial care *by examining* the connexion and former dealings *of the two parties*.

70. A document written *by the party himself* must be authenticated by *examining* the writing, an attested *document must be authenticated* by *examining* the witnesses. Witnesses are overruled by documents, not documents by witnesses.

71. If a document is split in two, or torn, or stolen, or effaced, or destroyed, or badly written, another document must be executed. This is the rule regarding documents.

---

## V. Chapter.

### *On Evidence by Witnesses and on the Ordeal by Balance.*

1. In doubtful cases, when there are two conflicting parties, the facts have to be ascertained by *the deposition of* witnesses, as to what was seen, heard, or understood by them.

2. He has to be considered as a witness who has witnessed a deed with his ears or eyes; with his ears, if the perpetrator of the deed has been speaking; with his eyes, if he has been committing an action.

3. Eleven descriptions of witnesses are recognised in law by the learned, five of which are made, and the remaining six are not made.

4. A witness by record, by memory, by accident, by secrecy, and by corroboration, these are the five classes of made witnesses.

5. But the witnesses not made have been declared by the wise to be six-fold, of which three are not appointed.

6. The fellow-villagers, a judge, a king, one authorized to manage the affairs of the parties, one deputed by the claimant,

7. In family disputes persons of the same family, shall be witnesses. A smaller number of witnesses than three is objectionable, and they should be blameless, decent, and intelligent persons.

8. They may be either *Brahmins*, or *Vaiçyas*, or *Kshatriyas*, or else unimpeachable *Çúdras*. Each of these shall be witness for persons of his own order, or for any order, *if there are no witnesses of the same order*.

9. Among companies of artisans, men who are artisans shall be witnesses; and men of one tribe among those of the same; foresters among those living outside; and women among women.

10. And if in any association, etc., any one falls out *with his associates*, he shall not bear testimony with regard to them; for they are all his enemies.

11. The incompetent witnesses too have in the law-

books been declared by the learned to be of five sorts, by reason of interdict, of delinquency, of contradiction, of voluntary deposition, and of intervening decease.

12. Learned *Brahmins*, etc., by interdict; thieves, etc., if their delinquency has become public; by reason of contradiction, *i.e.* if there is no agreement between the witnesses in a law-suit.

13. Voluntary deposition is when a man comes and offers his evidence without having been asked to do so. Incompetent by intervening decease are *all witnesses* after the death of the claimant, except those instructed by him on the point of death.

14. Learned *Brahmins*, ascetics, superannuated persons, and religious devotees, are those incapacitated by interdict; there is no other reason given for it.

15. Thieves, public offenders, violent persons, gamblers, murderers, are incompetent from delinquency; there is no truth in them.

16. If the statements of witnesses, who have been summoned by the king for the decision of an action, do not agree, they are rendered incompetent by contradiction.

17. He who, without having been appointed, comes and offers his evidence, is termed a spy in the law-books; he is not worthy to bear testimony.

18. How can any person bear testimony, if the claimant is no longer in existence, whose claim should have been heard? Such a person is an incompetent witness by reason of intervening decease.

19. If both parties in a dispute have witnesses, the witnesses of that party shall be heard which has brought forward the claim.

20. In such cases only, where the claimant is worsted in the trial, the witnesses of the defendant have to be examined.

21. For the defendant answers word for word to the charge brought forward by his adversary; and indicating *every* error *in the assertions of the latter* he points out the true *state of the case.*

22. No one should secretly confer with a witness summoned by his adversary, neither should he cause him to differ with another: a person resorting to such practices loses his suit.

23. If a witness dies or goes abroad after having received the summons, those who have heard his deposition, may give evidence; for a second-hand statement is evidence *also.*

24. Even after a great lapse of time a written document does not lose its validity; if a man can write, he should commit it to writing himself; if he cannot *write himself,* he should not cause it to be written *by others.*

25. The deposition of a witness by record remains valid up to the eighth year, that of a witness come by accident remains valid up to the fifth year.

26. The deposition of a secret witness remains valid up to the third year; the deposition of a witness by corroboration is declared to lose its validity after one year.

27. Or no definite period is adhered to in judging *the validity of* a deposition; for those learned in law have said that testimony depends upon memory.

28. He whose intellect, memory, or hearing, has

never been deranged, may give valid evidence even after a very considerable lapse of time.

29. But six different kinds of law-cases have been indicated by the wise, in which witnesses are not concerned; evident signs take in these cases the place of the deposition of witnesses.

30. One *taken with* a firebrand in his hand is manifestly an incendiary; one *taken with* a weapon in his hand is known to be a murderer; if a man *and another man's wife* are seen to play with one another's hair, the man must be an adulterer.

31. One who goes about with a hatchet in his hand, is a destroyer of bridges; one who is carrying an axe, is a destroyer of trees.

32. One covered with hideous marks * is a public offender. In *all* such cases witnesses are superfluous; only in the *last-mentioned* case of violence close scrutiny is required.

33. Some one might make marks upon his person on purpose to injure an enemy. *Therefore* persons of acute perception should investigate such cases.

34. One interested in the subject matter, a friend, a servant, an enemy, one perjured, a sick, or infamous person, cannot be made witnesses.

35. The king cannot be made a witness, nor mean artificers, nor public dancers and singers, nor a slave, nor a cheat, nor one exhausted, nor a *decrepit* old man, nor a woman, nor a child, nor a potter.

36. Nor *can the following persons be made* witnesses: one intoxicated, a madman, a negligent or distresed

* "Blood and the like," says Raghunandana, who quotes and explains this passage, Vyavahàratattva, p. 54; cf. Vîr. 223.

person, one extremely grieved, a gamester, a village priest, one who is gone out upon a long pilgrimage, one engaged in transmarine commerce, an ascetic, a scholar;

37. One deformed, one person only, a learned *Brahmin*, a man of a vile class, an eunuch, a public dancer or singer,* an atheist, a *Vrátya*, one who has deserted his wife or his *holy* fire, one who makes illicit offerings;

38. One who eats from the same dish *as the defendant in a law-suit*, a servant,† a member of the highest class, kinsmen, one formerly perjured, a dancer,‡ one who lives by *selling* poison (?), a snake-catcher;

39. A poisoner, an incendiary, a butcher, the son of a *Çúdrá*, one excluded from society, one oppressed by fatigue, a public offender, one exhausted,‡ one who has suffered his fire to go out;

40. One who associates with people of wicked habits, an idiot, a seller of oil or roots, one who is possessed by a demon, an enemy of the king, weather-prophets, and astrologers;

41. A juggler, an avaricious or cruel person, enemies of a company *of merchants*, or an association *of kinsmen*, an irreligious man, one self-sold, one who has a limb too little, a *Bhagavṛitti*;

42. One who has bad nails or black teeth, a leper, one who betrays his friends, an idiot, a seller of spirits, a murderer, a leather manufacturer, a lame man, an outcast, a forger;

* This is a repetition, cf. 35.

† Repeated from 34.

‡ See above, 34, 35, 37.

43.* An impostor, one who has eaten too much (?) † a robber, a follower of the king;

44. One who sells men, animals, meat, bones, honey, milk, water, or butter, a *Brahmin*, and a member of a twice-born class, who is guilty of usury;

45. A man sprung from a good family, who neglects the duties of his class, a panegyrist, one who serves low people, one who quarrels with his father, and a mischief-maker.

46. Nor a child, a woman, one man alone, an evil-doer, relatives, and enemies, because they would bear false testimony.‡

47. A child would speak falsely from ignorance, a woman from levity, an evil-doer from habitual depravity, relatives from affection, enemies from desire of revenge.

48. By consent of both litigants even a single person may be a witness, and must be examined before the court.

49. One who oppressed by the conscience of his guilt looks as if he was ill, is *constantly* shifting his position, and runs after every man;

50. Who suddenly coughs without reason, and draws repeated sighs; who scratches as if writing with his feet, and who shakes his arm and clothes;

51. Whose countenance changes colour, whose forehead sweats, and whose lips become dry; who looks above and about him;

52. Who talks a great deal without restraint, like a

* See Appendix.

† *Pratyavasita*; see Böthlingk-Roth's Dictionary, s. v.

‡ Repeated from 34 and the following Çlokas.

man in haste, and without being asked, such a person is manifestly a false witness, and should receive severe punishment.

53. The above-mentioned persons, slaves, impostors, and the like, shall nevertheless be admitted to bear testimony, with *due* consideration of the weight of the case in hand.

54. In all cases of violence, theft, adultery, and both kinds of insult, the witnesses should not be scrutinized.

55. He who does not give his evidence, although he has related *what he knows* to others, deserves extreme punishment; for he is worse than a false witness.

56. If a witness speaks falsely through covetousness, he shall be fined a thousand *paṇas*; if through distraction of mind, *two hundred and fifty, or* the lowest amercement; if through terror, the middling amercement; if through friendship, four times the lowest;

57. If through lust, ten times the lowest amercement; if through wrath, three times the next *or middlemost;* if through ignorance, two hundred complete; if through inattention, a hundred only.

58. *The judge,* having summoned the witnesses, and bound them down firmly by an oath, shall examine them separately, all of them familiar with the rules of duty and acquainted with the circumstances of the case.

59. Let him cause a priest to swear by his veracity, a *Kshatriya* by his horse or elephant and his weapons, a *Vaiçya* by his kine, grain, or gold, a *Çúdra* by all *possible* crimes.

60. By ancient holy texts, which extol the pre-eminence of truth and denounce falsehood, let him inspire them with deep awe.

61. Human nature *being perverse* cannot be got rid of except through strict morality; *consequently* a witness who speaks the truth in giving evidence will obtain splendid places of abode *hereafter*, and the highest fame here below; such testimony is revered by *Brahma* himself.

62. He who speaks falsely will enter his enemy's house, naked, with his head shorn, tormented with hunger and thirst, deprived of his sight, to beg food with a potsherd.

63. He who speaks falsely is tied closely with *Varuṇa's* fetters, and has to enter, in a hundred new births, the bodies of vile creatures.

64. Whatever places of *torture* have been prepared for the slayer of a priest, for the murderer of a woman or child, for the injurer of a friend, and for an ungrateful man, those places are ordained for him who speaks falsely.

65. Shut out from the town and suffering hunger out of doors, shall he who gives false evidence constantly meet his enemies.

66. A false witness shall spend his nights in the same manner as a wife who has been superseded *by another*, or as a man who has been worsted in playing at dice, or as one whose body is weighed down by a *heavy* load.

67. A witness who gives evidence devoid of falsehood, frees himself from a thousand of *Varuṇa's* cords.

68. After the lapse of a hundred years one cord is

taken off from him; when he is free from the stain of sin, he becomes a woman.

69. Thus men are freed from this fetter after a fixed number of years.*

70. *Now* I shall state in a just enumeration in order, how many kinsmen a giver of false evidence kills *by his falsehood.*

71. He kills one generation or two by false testimony concerning rice or grain, three by false testimony concerning a vehicle, four by false testimony concerning beasts for draught;

72. He kills five by false testimony concerning cattle *in general;* he kills ten by false testimony concerning kine; he kills a hundred by false testimony concerning horses; and a thousand by false evidence concerning a human being;

73. He kills the born and the unborn by giving false evidence in a cause concerning gold; he kills everything by speaking falsely with regard to land; beware then of giving false evidence with regard to land.

74. Truth is said to be the one unequalled instrument of purification, the ladder by which *human beings* ascend to heaven, as a ferry *takes them* from one bank of a river to the other.

75. For truth ranks higher than a thousand horse-sacrifices. A cistern is better than a hundred wells, an offering better than a hundred cisterns,

76. A son better than a hundred offerings, and truth better than a hundred sons. It is truth which makes

* 69–71 has been translated literally from the MSS.; however, half a Çloka seems wanting between 69 and 70, not to mention other difficulties of this somewhat obscure passage.

the earth bear *all beings,* truth which makes the sun rise.

77. He whose mind is persistent in truth, obtains a divine state even in this world. Speak the truth and abandon falsehood; it is through truth that thou wilt obtain heaven.

78. Truth makes the wind blow, Truth makes the water flow, Truth is the greatest boon, there is no kind of austerity so effective as Truth.

79. *To speak the* truth is the highest duty in the world, this is what has been revealed to us; the gods are perfect Truth, the human race is Falsehood.

80. By neglecting Truth thou wilt precipitate thyself into a most dreadful, hellish abode. And in the hells the powerful and cruel ministers of *Yama*

81. Will cut off thy tongue and constantly strike thee with swords and pierce thee with spears, while thou art wailing incessantly.

82. When thou art standing, they will fell thee to the ground and throw thee into the fire. Having thus borne with pain the tortures of hell for a long time,

83. Thou shalt in this world enter the *vile* bodies of crows, vultures, and the like. Being aware of these evils, with which Falsehood, and, on the other hand, of the *aforesaid* advantages, with which Truth is attended,

84. A witness should speak the truth at once, readily, and not commit himself. No relatives, no friends, no treasures, be they ever so great,

85. Are able to hold him back by the hand, who is about to dive into the tremendous darkness *of Hell.* Thy ancestors are in suspense when thou art come to give evidence, *and ponder in their mind:*

86. "Wilt thou deliver us *from Hell,* or precipitate us

*into it?"* Truth is the soul of man, everything depends upon Truth,

87. Therefore *strive to* acquire a better self by speaking the truth. Thy whole lifetime, from the night in which thou wert born up to the night in which thou wilt die,

88. Has been spent in vain if thou givest false evidence. There is no higher virtue than veracity, nor is there a greater crime than falsehood;

89. One must speak the truth therefore, especially when asked to bear testimony. There are two ancient, fine Çlokas relating to this very subject.

90. "If a base wretch speaks a lie in the cause of another, what baseness is there which may not be expected from such a man, fearless of Hell, when he is himself engaged in a law-suit?

91. All *human* concerns are based upon words, have words for their roots, and spring from words; he who steals good words *and violates the truth*, is capable of committing any theft *or other crime*."

92. If there be contradictory evidence, the plurality of witnesses decides the case; if the number of witnesses on both sides in a law-case is found to be equal, *the defendant* must be absolved.

93. The deposition of the witnesses loses its validity in this case on account of the subtlety of evidence by witnesses. But if a litigant is, by the act of fate, abandoned by his witnesses in a law-suit,

94. The wise will not have him absolved even through an ordeal. If a witness gives unmeaning evidence, *the deposition of* the appointed *witnesses* being full of meaning,* his testimony is *as good as* ungiven.

* ? *arthajáteshu.* Cf. Böthl. R. s. v. i. 435. v. 1045.

95. If the witnesses were to disagree with one another as to place, time, age, matter, usages, tribe, or class,

96. Such depositions, too, are worthless. If the witnesses name too low or too high *a sum*,

97. This too must be known to make no evidence. This is the rule of witnesses.

98. If, owing to the negligence of the creditor, both a written contract and witnesses are missing, and the defendant denies his obligation, three kinds of measures may be had recourse to:

99. Repeated admonitions, subtle ratiocination (*yuktileça*), and, thirdly, an oath: these are the measures which *a judge* should successively resort to.

100. He who does not refute his adversary's statements, though he has been called upon to do so repeatedly, three or four or five times, will consequently be bound to pay the debt.

101. If the defendant has resisted such an admonition, he shall aggress him by subtle ratiocination founded upon place, time, and matter, upon the connexions *of the party*, circumstantial evidence, the nature of the case, and so forth.

102. If reasonable inference (*yukti*) also leads to no result, let him cause the defendant to undergo one of the ordeals, by fire, water, *proof of* virtue, and so forth, according to the time of the year and to the strength of the defendant.

103. He whom the blazing fire burns not, whom the water soon forces not up, or who meets with no speedy misfortune, must be held veracious in his testimony on oath.

104. Let ordeals be administered if an offence has

been committed in a solitary forest, at night, in the interior of a house, and in cases of violence, and of denial of a deposit.

105. He is freed from the charge; otherwise he is guilty.*

106. The same rule holds good in regard to women accused of *bad* morals, in cases of theft and robbery, and in all cases of denial of an obligation.

107. I shall now state the rule of ordeals, as it has been laid down by *Manu,* for the four classes severally.†

108. By the gods and the *Ṛishis* themselves oaths have been taken. *Vasishta* took an oath, being accused of practising witchcraft.

109. The seven *Ṛishis,* rich in austerities and inflexible, took an oath before *Indra* on account of *Pushkara,* in order to clear themselves mutually *of suspicion.*

110. The balance, fire, water, poison, and sacred libation are said to be the five divine tests for the purgation of suspected persons.

111. *Nárada* has formerly proclaimed *these ordeals* as a test in doubtful cases, when strong-minded persons labour under a charge, in order that right might be discerned from wrong.

112. The balance, and the other divine tests which have been ordained by the sages, should be adminis-

* This detached hemistich is apparently an interpolation; it may have been added by some one to 103 as a gloss.

† The following section on ordeals is the most difficult portion of the work. The style is so short and partly even obscure, that it seems as if this was a mere extract from the numerous Çlokas on the same subject, which are quoted as Nárada's in the Víramitrodaya, Mitákshará, and Raghunandana's Divyatattva.

tered by the king with the assent of the claimant, not without it.

113. If he administers them in any other manner, he is as guilty as a thief. *The ordeal by* fire is ordained for the rainy season, *the ordeal by* balance for the autumn season.

114. *The ordeal by* water is ordained for the hot season, *the ordeal by* poison *should be administered* in very cold weather. The balance is destined for the *Brahmin*, fire is declared for the *Kshatriya*,

115. Water is destined for the *Vaiçya*, the *Çúdra* should be tested by poison. *The judge* should not administer poison to the *Brahmin*, nor should a *Kshatriya be compelled to* take the iron *ball*.

116. Let *the judge* administer the ordeals by fire, water, and poison to strong men only, and let him always administer the ordeal by balance to children, to superannuated persons, and to those who are unsound in mind (*atura*).

117. Purgation should not be by water in the cold season; nor should purgation be by fire in the warm season; nor should poison be administered during the rainy season; nor the balance in very windy weather.

118. Let *the judge* keep away fire from leprous persons, water from the asthmatic, and let him keep away poison from those afflicted with bile and phlegm.

119. I shall state next the excellent rule of the ordeal by balance, and how the king and chief judge should administer it to a man.

120. The two posts of the balance should be four hands high above *the ground; the beam of the* balance

should be made five hands long, and the *argalá or transverse beam* * two hands long.

121. The *beam of the* balance should be made four hands long,† equitable, and having the required qualities. Having made a wooden *beam of the* balance,

122. An honest man should connect it with the *two scales of the balance* and fasten it, after it has been made to fit well, in an east-western direction. Goldsmiths, skilful traders, and braziers,

123. Who are familiar with the practice of weighing, should examine the balance. The two strings having been fastened in the two strong rings of the balance,

124. The person should be put into the one scale, and a stone should be put into the other. Having weighed the man, *the judge* should make a proper mark for both *scales* on the receptacle of *each* scale (*kakshástháne*); ‡

125. Then he should cause the man to descend

* *Argalá* properly means a pin or a bar; but here it is evidently used to denote what other lawgivers call the *aksha*, *i.e.*, the transverse beam fixed to the two posts. Our author himself makes use of the latter expression below 130.

† This rule directly contradicts the preceding one as to the length required for the beam of the balance. The whole of this hemistich seems to be an interpolation substituted for another hemistich, which must have contained particulars regarding the scales of the balance.

‡ This term appears to be synonymous with what other legislators denote as the *toraṇas*, *i.e.*, the bows, upon which a chalk-mark is made in the same height as the scales, in order to facilitate a comparison between the results of the first and of the second weighing. See the drawing of a balance in Stenzler's Essay, 'Die indischen Gottesurtheile,' Zeitschr. d. d. morg. gs. ix. 661.

from the balance, an experienced man should pay his reverence to it *by putting* perfumes and flowers *into it*;

126. And having adjured the balance by imprecations, *the judge* should cause the person *accused* to be placed in the balance again.

127. "O balance, thou only knowest what mortals do not comprehend. This man being arraigned in a cause, is weighed upon thee.

128. Therefore mayest thou deliver him lawfully from this perplexity." Then the king should have him placed into the balance, and the proceeding takes its course.

129. Should the individual increase in weight, he is not innocent; if he be equal in weight, or lighter, his innocence is established.

130. In case of the strings bursting, or of the splitting of the transverse beam (*aksha*), the person *accused* should be placed in the scale once more. Thus the facts will be put beyond the reach of doubt, and a just sentence be the result.

---

## VI. Chapter.

### *Of the Ordeal by Fire.*

1. Now I shall state the excellent rule of the ordeal by fire, how the king should administer it to persons persistent in *their denial of* the charge.

2. A man should first make seven circles. It has

been ordained, that thirty-two inches should be between one circle and another.

3. Thus the seven circles *will cover* a space of two hundred and twenty-four inches of land in measurement.

4. But the breadth of *each* circle shall be made equal to the foot of him for whose justification the ordeal has been instituted.*

5. The circles having been smeared *with cow-dung and so forth,* the man, who must have fasted and *made himself* clean, shall turn his face towards the east or west, stretch out both arms,

6. And shall have seven *açvattha* leaves *laid upon his hands and fastened upon them* afterwards with strings, and take a smooth ball of red-hot iron, fifty *palas* by weight, in his hands,

7. And slowly walk through the seven circles. Having reached the seventh circle, he shall put down the ball upon the ground.

8. If he be burnt, his guilt is proved; but if he remain wholly unburnt, he is undoubtedly innocent.

9. If he let the ball drop from fear, or if there exist a doubt as to whether he is burnt *or not,* let him take the iron again, in order that the ordeal may be terminated.

10. "Thou, O fire, dwellest in the interior of all creatures, like a witness. Thou only knowest what mortals do not comprehend.

11. This man is arraigned in a cause and desires

* *i.e.,* the breadth of a circle *without the space between two circles.* This seems to be a special rule for such cases where the foot of the accused is longer than 16 inches (*angulas*); see Stenzler, l. c. 669, Mit. 151.

acquittal. Therefore mayest thou deliver him lawfully from this perplexity."

---

## VII. Chapter.

### *Of the Ordeal by Water.*

1. Now I shall proclaim the excellent rule of the ordeal by water. Persons labouring under suspicion should dive into water.

2. The water *in this kind* of ordeals should be very clear, very cool, free from leeches and mud, broad, and not too shallow.

3. *The person* shall enter into the water up to his navel, but he should avoid diving deeper than that. *Another man* shall discharge three arrows from a moderate bow.

4. A strong bow is 700 feet, a moderate bow 600, an inferior bow 500 angulas long: this is the rule of the bow.

5. *But* if the arrows have been discharged from a very strong or very inferior bow, one shall assign a space of 64 feet for him *who has to discharge the arrows.*

6. If the arrows have been discharged in the right manner (? *sthite tu váṇa-sampáte*) a skilful and honourable man of a twice-born class, who is a swift runner, should be chosen, *and enjoined to fetch one, the accused diving under water in the mean time.*

7. Having worshipped the deities *Yama* and *Varuṇa,* he shall dive under water which has no strong current.

8. This proceeding shall be superintended by thoroughly honest persons, who know the rules of the law-code and are free from both love and hatred.

9. But if, while the second arrow having been discharged is brought back by a strong man, he continues under water, he obtains acquittal.

10. Otherwise he is guilty, though only one limb of his have been seen; or he shall dive down in another place than that where he first dived.

11. The trial not having been decided, an experienced man shall again make him dive under the water, in order that the judges may be enabled without fail to distinguish right from wrong.

12. If only his ear, eye, face, or nose become visible, while he is standing in the water, he is guilty; he obtains acquittal, if he is not seen *at all.*

13. Women must not be compelled to undergo *this ordeal,* nor men of feeble constitution; it is on account of their timidity that women are exempted, feeble men on account of their incapacity to bear fatigue.

14. " Because fire arose from water, therefore those who know the precepts of the law ordain purgation to be made especially by water.

15. Thou art exalted over all gods and the best means of purification; thou art the producer of creatures, O mighty, pleasant, cool water.

16. Thou, O water, livest in the interior of all creatures like a witness; thou knowest what men do not comprehend.

17. This man, arraigned in a cause, dives into thee; therefore mayest thou deliver him lawfully from this perplexity."

## VIII. Chapter.

### *Of the Ordeal by Poison.*

1. Now I shall declare the excellent rule of *the ordeal by* poison, how the king should administer poison, the most effective means of purification for a person *accused.*

2. One acquainted with the law should not *administer it* either at noon, or in the afternoon, or in the twilight, and further avoid *the ordeal by poison* in autumn, summer, spring, and the rainy season.

3. Roasted poison, poison which has been spoiled by shaking it, scented, and mixed poison, and the *Kálakúṭa* and *Alambú* poisons should be carefully avoided.

4. Poison from the horn of an animal or poison produced on the *Himálaya* mountains should be chosen, which is first rate and has *the required* flavour, colour, and taste. It should be given in the manner stated, at the beginning of winter.

5. [Seven-eighths of a twentieth of a sixth of a *pala* (= 960 *yavas*)* of the poison (*i.e.* seven yavas of poison) should be administered,] mixed with clarified

* $\frac{1}{6} \cdot \frac{1}{20} \cdot \frac{7}{8} \cdot 960$ *yavas*=7 *yavas*; see the prescriptions of other legislators, Stenzler, l.c. 674. The MSS. being quite corrupted here, the above clause has been substituted for the words of the text.

butter, to the accused who must have fasted, in the presence of the gods and of *Brahmins*.

6. "Thou, O poison, art the son of *Brahma*, thou art persistent in truth and justice; relieve this man from sin, and by thy virtue become as ambrosia to him.

7. On account of thy venomous and dangerous nature thou art the destruction of all living creatures; thou art destined to show the difference between right and wrong like a witness.

8. Thou knowest the good actions and the conduct of men, whether it be good or bad, *in short* whatever men do not comprehend.

9. This man is arraigned in a cause and wishes to obtain acquittal; therefore mayest thou lawfully deliver him from this perplexity."

10. If the poison is digested easily, without violent symptoms, the king shall recognise him as innocent, and dismiss him after having honoured him with presents.

---

## IX. Chapter.

### *Of the Ordeal by Sacred Libation.*

1. I shall proclaim next the excellent rule of the ordeal by sacred libation. The sacred libation is ordained to be used in the morning by a person fasting, having bathed, clothed in moist garments,

2. And not in low spirits or in distress. *The judge* should give the accused *water in which an image of*

that deity to whom he is devoted *has been bathed*, thrice calling out the charge, with composure.

4. One to whom any calamity or misfortune happens within a week or a fortnight, is proved to be guilty.

5. He shall pay the creditor the debt he owes him, and the king shall exact from him a fine to the double amount of his debt.

6. The ordeal by sacred libation should be avoided in case of a great offender, or one who leads an immoral life, or a murderer, or an eunuch, or a vile man, or an atheist, or one who has an unclean occupation.

7. *The ordeal by* water must not be administered to persons of feeble constitution, nor *the ordeal by* poison to men who have a bad liver, nor should *a judge* administer the ordeal by fire to lame, blind, crippled, or idiotic persons.

8. *The accused* shall touch the heads of priests or take grains of rice into his mouth; in heavy charges the ordeal by sacred libation should be avoided.

# [PART II.—LAWS.]

## THE HEAD OF DISPUTE, CALLED "RECOVERY OF A DEBT." *

---

### II. HEAD OF DISPUTE.

*On Deposits.*

1. Where a man entrusts any of his effects with another, in whom he has confidence, without enter-

* The insertion of this heading is apparently meant to imply that the "Recovery of a Debt" ought to have been treated in this place, as the first head of dispute, instead of in the 3rd chapter of the first part (see p. 15). In other works also the place assigned to the rules regarding loans varies a great deal: thus in Yájnavalkya's law-code, and therefore also in the Mitákshará, the section on Recovery of a Debt precedes the section on evidence by witnesses, documents, and divine test; in Manu, Book viii., the same subject is in part mixed up with the rules of judicial procedure; in the Víramitrodaya, Vivádachintámani and Vyavahâramayúkha, on the other hand, the section on debts is treated as the first title of law, and apart from the judicatory. These facts are significant enough: so pre-eminent was at first the redress for non-payment among the motives for going to law, that

taining any doubt *as to the recovery of his property,* it is termed deposit, a head of dispute.

2. When one article hidden in another, *as for instance in a basket,* is deposited, without mentioning *its kind and form,* in another man's house, it is considered as an *aupanidhika* deposit.

3. *A deposit* is again declared to be of two sorts, attested and unattested. It must be restored in the same condition *in which it was delivered;* otherwise *the depositary* shall be tried by ordeal.

4. He who does not return a deposit on demand of the depositor, shall be fined by the king; and, if it be lost, shall pay its value.

5. And he who derives gain *from the deposit,* without the depositor's consent, shall be fined and pay the value of the thing, with interest.

6. If a man is sued for more than one article, and denies the possession of all, he must surrender all, though he be only proved to possess one.

7. What is lost, together with the property of the depositary, is lost to the depositor; so if it be lost by the act of fate or the king, unless there was a fraudulent act *on the part of the depositary.*

8. The same rule holds good with regard to loans for use (*yáchita*), deposits for delivery (*anváhita*), bailments with an artist, a deposit unspecified (*nyása*), and a mutual trust.

9. If a man privately receive a fine, or a valuable commodity, the law is the same in that case; these are declared to be the six sorts of deposits.

the rules regarding it became strictly interwoven with the laws of judicial procedure in general, and were not separated from them, till, in the middle ages, the systematizing spirit of the Hindu lawyers would no longer bear with this fusion.

## III. Head of Dispute.

### *Concerns among Partners.*

1. When traders, or others, jointly carry on business, it is called a Concern among Partners, a head of dispute.

2. The junction of stock is the basis of *the transactions of* men carrying on business jointly with a view to gain; therefore each should contribute his share *to the common exertion*.

3. The charges, loss, and profit of each *partner* are *either equal to those of the rest or smaller or greater than theirs,* according as his share is equal or more or less.

4. Let the partners, faithful to their agreement,* duly contribute to the stock, to the charges of living and of trade, to the deductions and weights, and the care of valuable articles.

5. Each *member* has to make good what has been lost by *his* want of care, and † if he has acted against the will of, or without authorization from, all partners.

6. He who preserves, by his own effort, the goods of the partnership, when a calamity arises from Fate,

* Colebrooke translates the same clause (*samaye sve vyavasthitáḥ*) somewhat freely: "unless bound by a *previous* agreement;" see Dig. ii. 3, vii., where this passage is quoted.

† Omitted in Colebrooke's translation, ibid. xiii.

from robbers, or from the king, is entitled by law to a tenth part of them.

7. Should one partner meet with a calamity, his heir shall undertake the work; or, if there be no heir, another *partner*, who is able *to do it*; or, *if there be no such person*, all *the partners*.

8. When an *officiating* priest has been disabled, another *priest* shall perform his work, and receive from him the stipulated share of his fee.

9. Both the priest who abandons a sacrificer, though he be no offender nor otherwise faulty, and the sacrificer who abandons a priest, who is no offender, shall be punished.

10. *Officiating* priests are of three sorts, hereditary, appointed by *the sacrificer* himself, and he who voluntarily officiates for friendship's sake.

11. This is the law for hereditary priests and for those who are appointed by *the sacrificer* himself; but there is no offence in abandoning a priest who officiates of his own accord.

12. A merchant should in passing by a toll-house pay the toll, which has been fixed; no wise man should neglect to do so, it is called *the king's* due.

13. He who avoids a toll-house, he who buys or sells at any other than the ordinary time, and he who makes a wrong estimate in declaring the value *of his property*, shall pay eight times the amount of his gain.

14. Should a travelling merchant, who has come from abroad, meet his death, the king shall keep his goods and chattels till the heir makes his appearance.

15. Should he have no heir, let the king deliver it to his relatives or remoter kindred; and if no such make their appearance, let him keep it well guarded for ten years.

16. Such property without an owner, and without *a claimant as* heir *to the deceased,* let the king, when it has been kept for ten years, appropriate to his own use: thus justice will not be violated.

---

## IV. Head of Dispute.

### *Recovery of a Gift.*

1. If any one wants to take back a gift which has not been made in due form, it is called Recovery of a Gift, a head of dispute.

2. The rule of gift is fourfold in law; what may be given and what not, valid and invalid gifts.

3. There are eight kinds of things that may not be given; what may be given is of one kind *only;* valid gifts are declared to be of seven sorts; invalid gifts assume sixteen forms.

4. An article bailed for delivery, a thing let for use, a pledge, joint property, a deposit, a son, a wife, the whole wealth of a man who has a son,

5. And, *of course,* that which has been promised to another, cannot, according to the saying of the sages, be given away even by a person who is in the extremity of distress.

6. What is left of the property, after the expenses for the maintenance of the family have been defrayed, may be given, *but* nothing beyond is to be touched; by doing thus you will fulfil the law.

7. Those conversant with the rules of gift consider as valid gifts the price delivered for a commodity sold, wages, *a fee given* for an amusement, *and gifts made* from natural affection, as an acknowledgment to a benefactor, as a nuptial present, and through regard.

8. What has been given by men agitated with fear, anger, sorrow, lust, or *the pain of* an illness, or as a bribe, or in jest, or by mistake, or in connexion with a fraudulent practice,

9. By a child, an idiot, a dependent, diseased, intoxicated, or insane person, an outcast, in consideration of a work to be performed, *if that work is not performed*, or from interested motives, must be considered as an invalid gift.

10. What has been given to an unworthy man from a wrong estimate of his character, for an illegal act, or from contempt, is likewise held to be a void gift.

11. Both he who accepts an invalid gift from avarice, and he who makes an illegitimate gift, shall be punished, as well as he who accepts illegitimate gifts, and he who covets invalid gifts.

## V. Head of Dispute.

### *Breach of Promised Obedience.*

1. If a man having promised to perform *any kind of* service does not perform it, it is termed Breach of Stipulated Obedience, a head of dispute.

2. The learned have mentioned in law five kinds of persons bound to obedience;' four of these are *free* labourers, *the fifth kind, namely,* the slaves are again of fifteen sorts.

3. A pupil, an apprentice, a hired servant, and, in the fourth place, an agent, are the *free* labourers; slaves are those born in the house, and so forth.

4. The learned have said that all these owe *a certain degree of* dependence; but their respective rank and wages depend on their caste and the work they do.*

5. There are two kinds of work to be distinguished —pure and impure work. What is done by the servant is pure, and what is done by the slave, impure.

6. Clearing the house, the gateway, the convenience, and the road from rubbish, rubbing the secret limbs, and gathering and removing impurities, *especially* urine and fæces,

* Colebrooke, Dig. iii. 1, vii. "He is called a labourer by class, and has a distinct subsistence." This is an instance of the misapprehensions which the translation of disconnected Çlokas or hemistichs only, as is here the case, must necessarily lead to, if it is not made with reference to the context in which they stood.

7. Attending the master at his pleasure, and rubbing him, are to be considered as impure work, and all other *work* as pure.

8. A pupil shall obey his teacher till he has mastered science; he shall equally obey his master's wife and son.

9. A pupil shall collect alms, and take his food (*pali*) on a low seat, free from conceit. His couch shall be humble; and he shall salute *all those who live* in his teacher's house first, *when he meets them.*

10. He shall never appear before his teacher, or stay with him without his permission; and he shall unflinchingly do the work he has been bid to do, if he can.

11. He shall read in the proper time, and if he has not been forbidden to do so by his master; and sit at his master's feet or by his head in an attentive attitude.

12. His teacher shall reprimand him if he does not obey him; for *neglecting* his reading, he shall be chastised with a rope or the small shoot of a cane.

13. The teacher must not, in chastising and correcting him, beat him severely, nor on a noble part, nor on the breast; *by acting* otherwise the teacher becomes liable to punishment from the king.

14. Having finished his course of study, let him offer his leaving-present to his teacher and return home. These are the rules of conduct for a pupil.

15. Let him who wishes to acquire his art, with the assent of his kinsmen, reside with an instructor, after having fixed a certain period *of apprenticeship.*

16. The teacher shall instruct him, *keep him* in his own house, give him food, and not employ him in other work, but treat him as a son.

17. He who deserts a good instructor, who has given him *the benefit of* his teaching, shall be compelled by forcible means to stay with him, and is liable to whipping and confinement.

18. An apprentice must reside with his instructor till his time is out, even if he acquire his art *before the expiration of it.* As long as he is doing work there, his instructor shall take the profit of it.

19. Having acquired his art within the fixed time, the apprentice shall offer to the instructor the best reward in his power, and depart with his permission.

20. There are three classes of labourers, the highest, middle, and lowest class. The payment they get for their labour is fixed according to their proficiency, and to the benefit *derived from their exertions.*

21. The highest *class includes* soldiers; the middle *class,* servants employed in husbandry; the lowest *class,* carriers of burdens: such is the threefold division of labourers.

22. He to whom the management of business or the superintendence of the family is entrusted, is likewise to be reckoned among the *free* labourers; he is also termed family-servant.

23. These are the four descriptions of labourers who do pure work; all the rest do impure work, and are slaves, whereof there are fifteen kinds.

24. One born in the house, one bought, one received *by donation,* one got by inheritance, one maintained in a famine, one pledged by a *former* master,

25. One relieved from a great debt, one made prisoner in a war, one obtained through a wager, one who has offered himself, saying, "I am thine," an

apostate from religious mendicity, *a slave* for a fixed *period,*

26. One maintained in reward of the work performed by him, a slave for the sake of his wife, and one self-sold, are the fifteen kinds of slaves declared by the law.

27. Of these, the first four cannot be released from slavery, unless *they be emancipated* by the generosity of their masters. Their servitude is hereditary.

28. However, if a slave saves the life of his master, when he is in peril, he is released from slavery, and obtains a son's share.

29. One maintained in a famine is released from slavery on giving a pair of oxen; for what has been consumed in a famine is not discharged by labour *alone.*

30. One pledged is released when his master redeems him by paying the debt; but if *the creditor* takes him in place of payment, he becomes a purchased slave.

31. A debtor is released from bondage by the payment of his debt with interest; a slave for a fixed period after the expiration of such period.

32. One who has offered himself, saying, "I am thine"; one made prisoner in a war; and one obtained through a wager, recover their liberty on giving a substitute equally capable of labour.

33. An apostate from religious mendicity shall be the king's slave. He cannot be emancipated, *for* there is no atonement for his crime.

34. One maintained in consideration of work performed by him, is immediately released on relinquishing his subsistence; and a slave for the sake of his wife is emancipated if he separates himself from her.

35. The base man who, being independent, sells himself, is the vilest of slaves; he also cannot be released from slavery.

36. They who are stolen and sold by thieves, and they who are enslaved by force, shall be set free by the king. Their slavery is not admitted.

37. In the inverse order of the *four* classes, slavery is not legal, except in the case of one who violates his duty; *in this respect* the condition of a slave is held similar to *that of* a wife.

38. Over the slave who, though not being his own master, has offered himself, saying, "I am thine," the new master does not acquire *legal* dominion; the former owner may reclaim him if he likes.

39. Three persons, a wife, a slave, and a son, have no property; whatever they acquire belongs to him under whose dominion they are.

40. A benevolent man, who desires to emancipate a slave of his, shall take a vessel of water from off the shoulder of the slave and break it.

41. Sprinkling the head of the slave with water *from a vessel* containing rice and flowers, and thrice calling him free, *the master* should dismiss him with his face turned towards the east.

42. Thenceforward let *the slave* be called "one graced with the favour of his master." Food prepared by him may be eaten, and gifts accepted from him, and he is respected *by honourable men.*

---

## VI. Head of Dispute.

### *Non-payment of Wages.*

1. The rule and act of the payment and receipt of labourers' wages is given *next.* It is called Non-payment of Wages, a head of dispute.

2. An employer shall pay proportionate wages to the servant hired by him, at the beginning, middle, or end of the work, according to contract.

3. Where the amount of the wages has not been fixed by contract, *the servant of* a merchant, a herdsman, and a field-labourer, shall respectively get a tenth part of the profit *on goods sold,* of the milk, and of the grain.

4. The working utensils and whatever is entrusted *to servants* for their master's business, should be diligently preserved, not wickedly neglected.

5. *A labourer* who refuses to perform the work he has contracted for shall be compelled to do it, first paying him his wages; if he persist in his refusal after receiving his wages, he shall forfeit twice their amount.

6. *A servant* who has stipulated *wages for a journey,* but leaves the cart on the way, shall give a sixth part of those wages; and if he does not convey the freight to its destination, he shall forfeit his wages.

7. The owner of goods who hires a cart or beasts for draught and takes them not, shall be compelled

to pay a fourth part of the hire; or the full amount, if he leave them on the road.

8. A carrier also who refuses to carry his load forfeits his wages, but he must pay the double amount of them if, after having begun *to carry it*, he puts it down again.

9. If the load be damaged by the carrier's fault, whatever is lost he shall be compelled to make good, unless the injury happened by the act of Fate or the king.

10. A herdsman who tends a hundred cows shall annually have a calf three years old, and he who tends two hundred cows shall get a milch cow; *besides, the latter* shall have every eighth day the milk *of all the cows.*

11. *The cows* which a cowherd takes to pasture at day-break, he shall every evening return to their owner, when they have eaten grass and drunk water.

12. If a cow be in danger, let the herdsman protect her to the best of his power; but if he be unable *to protect her,* let him hasten and give notice to his master.

13. A herdsman who preserves not a cow from accidents, who gives no alarm, and informs not his master, *when she is in danger,* shall pay the value of her *to her owner,* and a fine to the king.

14. If a cow has strayed, been destroyed by reptiles, or killed by dogs, or has died *by falling* into a pit, owing to the carelessness of the herdsman, the value of her shall be paid by him.

15. If goats or sheep are attacked by wolves and the keeper does not go *to repel the attack,* he shall be responsible for every one of them which a wolf shall violently kill.

16. When robbers have carried it away although he gave alarm, he is not bound to make it good, provided he give notice to his master in a *proper* place and season.

17. By this rule shall disputes with every description of herdsmen be decided; and if any cows die, *the keeper* becomes free from responsibility by producing their tails and horns.

18. If a prostitute do not attend after having received her fee, she shall be fined twice the sum she may have taken; but if *her paramour* refuse to receive her, he shall only lose the money he advanced.

19. If a man unnaturally abuse a prostitute's person, or cause her to be approached by many, he shall be compelled to pay eight times the amount *promised*, and a fine of equal amount.

20. He who dwells in a house, which he built on the ground of another man, and for which he pays rent, shall take with him, when he leaves it, the thatch, the wood, and the bricks.

21. But if he live without paying rent on the ground of another without *the owner's* consent, he shall by no means, when he quits it, take away the thatch and the wood.

22. Things hired let the hirer give back when the time has elapsed; whatever is broken or lost, he shall make good, except in the case of *inevitable* accident.

## VII. Head of Dispute.

### *Sale Without Ownership.*

1. When a deposit, or the goods of another lost *by him* and found *by a stranger,* or effects stolen, are clandestinely sold, it must be considered as Sale without Ownership.

2. The owner, finding a thing which had been sold by a stranger, shall keep it. There is no offence in a sale publicly made, but to sell anything in secret is theft according to law.

3. He who buys anything from a slave who has no authority *to sell it* from his master, or from a wicked man, by force, in private, at an inadequate price, or at an unseasonable hour, is equally guilty with the vendor.*

4. Let not the purchaser keep the vendor concealed; on that man depends his own justification. If he act otherwise, he is equally guilty *with the vendor,* and shall suffer the punishment of a thief.

5. The rule in a case of sale without ownership is this that the seller must restore the thing to the owner, pay to the purchaser the price for which it was sold, and a fine to the king.

6. If a man finds a treasure which has been in

* Colebrooke Dig. ii, 2, xxxviii: "... becomes an accomplice of the man who stole it." The clause "by force" is not contained in his translation.

terred by another person, let him deliver it to the king; treasures found by men of any class belong to the king, except those *found* by *Brahmins.*

7. A *Brahmin,* too, having found a treasure, should quickly announce it to the king: he may enjoy it, if the king grants it to him; if he does not announce it *to the king,* he is a thief.

8. Even if a man finds property of his own which he had lost, he must inform the king of it; he may take it without incurring blame in this case; otherwise it would be wrong.

---

## VIII. Head of Dispute.

### *Non-delivery of a Thing Sold.*

1. If an article has been sold and is not delivered to the purchaser, though he has paid its price, it is called Non-delivery of a Thing Sold, a head of dispute.

2. Property in this world is of two kinds, immoveable and moveable; and, in the laws of purchase and sale, both are called vendible property.

3. The rule of its delivery and receipt is held by the wise to be six-fold: by tale, weight, measure, work, beauty, and splendour.

4. He who, having sold vendible property for a *just* price, does not deliver it to the purchaser, shall be compelled, if it be immoveable, to pay for any subsequent damage; and if moveable, for the use and profits of it.

5. Should the value of a thing be diminished *in the*

*interval, the purchaser* shall receive it together with the difference of the value. Such is the rule for persons who reside in the same place; but to those who trade to foreign countries, the foreign profit must be made good.

6. Should the thing sold be damaged, or burned, or carried away *in the interval,* the loss shall fall on the vendor, who failed to deliver it *in due time,* after having sold it.

7. He who, having shown *a specimen of property* free from blemish, delivers blemished property, shall be made to pay double the price *to the vendee,* and a fine to the same amount.

8. He who sells a commodity to one man, and delivers it to another, shall likewise pay double the price, and a fine to the same amount.

9. If a purchaser refuse to accept an article he has purchased, when it is offered, the vendor commits no offence if he sell it to another.

10. The above rules are applicable, where the price has been paid; but where it has not been paid, the vendor is not to blame if he delays the delivery, unless there have been a special agreement *as to the times of delivery and payment.*

11. It is with a view to gain, that the purchase and sale of any commodity is made by merchants; *that gain,* be it great or small, is in each case in proportion to the price.

12. Therefore let merchants sell their articles *at a fair price, fixed* according to place and season, and let them not act crookedly: this is the best way of dealing in mercantile business.*

* The first half of this Çloka has been literally translated

## IX. HEAD OF DISPUTE.

### *Rescission of Purchase.*

1. If a purchaser, after buying a commodity for a *just* price, is dissatisfied with his purchase, it is called Rescission of Purchase, a head of dispute.

2. If a man, having bought a commodity for a *just* price, should suspect that he had made a bad purchase, he may return it on that very day to the seller, unless it be diminished.

3. The purchaser who returns it on the second day *from the date of the purchase*, shall forfeit a thirtieth part of the price; on the third day, twice as much; after that it is *absolutely* his own *and cannot be returned.*

4. A purchaser ought first to examine a commodity, and to ascertain what is good and bad in it; when, after inspection and approbation, he has purchased it, he is not competent to return it to the vendor.

5. Milch cattle ought to be examined within three days; beasts of burden, within five; the examination of jewels, pearls, and coral must take place within seven days;

6. Of male slaves, within half a month; of female

above, whereas Colebrooke, Dig. iii. 3, xxxviii., following Chandeçvara's explanation, has: "*when a price has not been stipulated*, let some merchant fix it according to place and time."

*slaves*, within a month; of every description of seeds, within ten days; of iron and clothes, within one day.

7. A mantle that has been worn and is tattered and soiled, cannot be returned to the vendor if it has been purchased in that damaged state.

8. The value of apparel once washed is diminished an eighth part; twice *washed*, a fourth; thrice *washed*, a third; and four times washed, a half.

9. Afterwards a deduction of a quarter from the half-reduced value is successively made,* until the fringe be wasted, and the cloth tattered; *but* for tattered cloth there is no regular reduction.

10. All iron utensils are invariably forged in fire; thus, in making them, their value is diminished by exposure to the fire.

11. The value of gold is not diminished at all by such exposure; silver *loses* two *palas* in the hundred; lead and tin lose eight *palas* in the hundred.

12. In copper the diminution of value amounts to five *palas in the hundred*, so also for articles made of it; for ore there is no such rule, because of its being unlike the aforesaid metals.

13. Thus the loss and gain arising from working these stuffs has been propounded; of linen, cotton, and wool the gain amounts to ten *palas* in the hundred,

14. In case it is large tissue; of tissue of a middling quality it is five in the hundred; of refined tissue the gain is considered three *palas*.

15. Of tissue made of the hair of beasts and of

* Colebrooke, Dig. iii, 3, li. Borrodaile, May, vi. 8, where this hemistich is also quoted, has translated it differently, but wrongly.

mixed tissue the thirtieth part is lost; neither gain nor loss is produced in tissue made of silk or bark.

16. An experienced merchant should not, after having purchased an article, rescind his purchase; he ought to know the *possible* loss and gain of each article, and business *in general.*

---

## X. Head of Dispute.

### *Breach of Order.**

1. The *general* rule settled among irreligious men, citizens, and the like, is named order; the head of dispute *concerning offences against it,* is named Breach of Order.

2. Let the king maintain order among the associations of irreligious men, of citizens (*or* sectaries who detract from the authority of the Veda), of companies of

* The corresponding word in Sanskrit, *saṃvidvyatikrama* or the synonymous expression *samayasyá'napakarma*, has been generally translated by "Non-performance of Agreements," (see, for instance, the heading of B. iii. ch. ii., in Colebrooke's Digest, and Tagore p. 108 ff.), or occasionally by "breach of compact;" but it refers to a kind of *contrat social* much rather than to private agreements. Sicé, in his French translation of the Vyavahára-Crama-Sangraha (Pondichéry, 1857), has *manquement aux observances* for it. Ellis (quoted by Borrodaile in Stokes' H. L. B. p. 141.) makes mention of special courts, called *gaṇa*, *kula*, and *kulika*, which formerly used to take cognizance of *saṃvidvyatikrama*, *i.e.*, "all transgressions against the discipline and peculiar customs of the tribe or family."

artisans, traders, and soldiers, and of various tribes and the like, both in solitary places and in frequented spots.

3. Whatever be their duties, their occupation, and prescribed rules, and whatever be the conduct enjoined to them, that let *the king* approve.

4. Let him restrain them from acts which are injurious to his interests, which in their nature are vile, or which obstruct his affairs.

5. Let him not tolerate promiscuous assemblies *of persons of different rank*, military array without cause, and reciprocal injuries.

6. Those especially should be punished who infringe the rule of the association; they should undergo fear and terror, being avoided like diseased persons.

7. And if wicked acts, unauthorised by moral law, are actually attempted, let a king, who desires prosperity, repress them.

---

## XI. Head of Dispute.

### *Contests regarding Boundaries.*

1. If a dispute arises about a bridge, field, landmark, cultivated or uncultivated land, *or in general about the boundaries of* an estate, *it is named* a Contest regarding Boundaries.

2. The decision in a contest regarding the boundaries of an estate should be given by the neighbours, the inhabitants of a town or village, and the elders.

3. Those *whose fields are situated* near the borders

*of the village territory* and who live by cultivating them, herdsmen, fowlers, hunters, and other foresters,

4. Shall fix the boundaries, designing them by marks, *such as* bran, coal, bricks, wells, temples, trees;

5. Ants' hills, mounds of earth, channels, shrubs, and the like, that are visible *at a distance*; receptacles of water,* gardens, paths, and old bridges.

6. When *these* marks have been carried away by a stream, or lost or destroyed, *let law-suits concerning the land in question be decided*† by inference from the traces left *of the old landmarks*, and by previous possession.

7. Now if the neighbours should speak falsely in deciding a question of this kind, the king should inflict the middling amercement upon each of them.

8. The assembly, the elders, and the rest should severally be punished; they shall have to pay the amercement of the first degree for their false decision.

9. Let not one man *alone* fix the boundaries, however trustworthy he may be; this duty ought to be performed by many, on account of its responsibility.

10. If a man were to fix them alone, let him do so after having fasted, taking much care, wearing a chaplet of red flowers, and a red mantle, and putting earth on his head.

11. If there be no witnesses, and no landmarks either, the king himself shall fix the boundaries between two estates according to his pleasure.

12. Thus the rule has been propounded for contests

* For this special meaning of *Kedára*, see Böthlingk-Roth s. v.; if it was taken in its usual acceptation "field," we should have a field recommended as landmark between two fields.

† See Appendix.

regarding houses, gardens, ponds, temples, and the like, as well as the space intermediate between two villages.

13. If trees have grown upon the boundaries between two fields, the fruits and flowers of these trees shall be divided between the owners of the two fields.

14. Should the boughs *of trees* grown upon the field of one man fall upon the field of another man, they shall belong to the former, *not to the latter*, as they have not grown upon his field.

15. A public thoroughfare, a place dedicated to the gods, a street, and a path, must not be stopped up by a place for sweepings, a pit, a drain, a heap, or the like.

16. Those who do cause such stoppage, upon such persons let the king inflict the severest punishment.

17. A bridge in the middle of another man's field must not be objected to, *for* the benefit is great, and the damage small; *so that* a profit accrues from it over the loss.*

18. Bridges of two kinds are known, the one open and the other confined. When for the passage of water, it is open; that which is closed is for the stoppage.

19. Grain is not spoiled by irrigation, but by being put under water; inundation entails the same disadvantages as dry ground (?).†

* Borrodaile's (May. xv, 13) different translation of this passage is founded upon a different reading, which is also found Vír. 467 (*ced* for *ca*).

† This verse contains a technical term, *abhyudaka*, which is not found in any dictionary, and the exact meaning of which could not be ascertained; unfortunately, it is not quoted in any of the modern works.

20. If any one, without asking the owner, repair a bridge, built long before, but fallen into decay, he shall not enjoy the profits of it.

21. But after the death of the owner or his kindred, any one may, with the permission of the king, undertake to rebuild the bridge.

22. Otherwise he would only harm himself after the fashion of a *foolish* huntsman; his arrows are lost, because he shoots once more at one whom he has shot already.

23. If the proprietor of a field be disabled to cultivate it *by poverty*, or die, or disappear, and if the field be freely *and openly* cultivated by another, the latter shall get its produce.

24. Should the proprietor return while the field is being cultivated, he shall get it back by paying all the expenses incurred for its cultivation.

25. The proprietor shall receive an eighth part of the produce *annually* until seven years have elapsed; but when the eighth year comes on, he shall take back the field possessed by the cultivator.

26. A field that has not been cultivated for one year, is called *ardhakhila*, and that which lies uncultivated for three years is termed *khila;* but ground which has been waste for five years is no better than a desert.

27. A field which has unquestionably been possessed by three successive generations cannot be lost through its being possessed by a stranger, except if the king ordains it.*

* This Çloka, though found in both MSS., is apparently an interpolation. In the Law of Inheritance also (see below 13, 48) a verse belonging, like the above Çloka, to the doctrine of possession and its effect, is inserted in an improper place.

28. If grain be damaged by cows or the like breaking through a fence, the herdsman is in that case liable to punishment, if he did not restrain *the cattle* to the best of his power.

29. But if the grain be destroyed, together with the root, the owner of the land shall receive the same quantity *of grain or a corresponding sum of money from the proprietor of the cattle;* the herdsman shall be dismissed with blows; and his master shall pay a fine *to the king.*

30. A cow within ten days after her calving, a bull, horses, and elephants, should be carefully kept off; their owner is not responsible *for their trespasses.*

31. Let *the king* compel *the proprietor of* a cow which has done mischief to pay a fine of one *másha,* and of a female buffalo, two *máshas;* and let the fine for goats and sheep trespassing with its young be half a *másha.*

32. For elephants and horses no fine is allowed, since they are considered *to assist the king in* protecting his subjects; nor for a stray cow, nor for one which has recently brought forth young ones, nor for one which desires the male.

33. For cattle abiding *until they be satisfied* the fine is double; but for cattle remaining *during the whole night* it is quadruple; and the punishment of theft is ordained for those herdsmen who, in their own sight, graze cattle on a stranger's ground.

34. If a cow, straying by fault of the herdsman, enters a field, no penalty is in that case exacted from the owner; the herdsman is to be punished for that *offence.*

35. If he be seized by the king or by a crocodile, struck by thunder and lightning, bitten by a serpent, fallen from a tree,

36. Smitten by a tiger and so forth, or afflicted with any disease, the herdsman deserves no blame; nor is his master responsible *for any mischief done by his cattle in the mean time.*

37. Every one who demands compensation for grain consumed by cows, shall receive that quantity of grain which, in the opinion of his neighbours, has been consumed there.

38. Grass must be made good to its owner, and grain to the husbandman; a fine is also ordained if corn be trodden by cows.

39. If *grain in* an unfenced field, which is situated close by a village or pasture land, or near the highway, has been destroyed, there is no offence on the part of the herdsman.

40. Towards the highway a fence should be made, over which a camel could not look, which cattle or horses could not overleap, and which a boar could not break through.

41. A well-kept house and field are the two bases upon which the *existence of* householders rests; therefore let not the king neglect them, for they are the support of householders.

42. According as the subjects of a king thrive or get into trouble, his merits and his treasure will increase or diminish; let him therefore act *up to this maxim,* considering that he will promote his *own* prosperity thus.

## XII. Head of Dispute.

### *Duties of Man and Wife.*

1. The rules for men and women concerning marriage and so forth are contained in the head of dispute, which is called Duties of Man and Wife.

2. Previous to the union of wife and man the betrothal takes place; the betrothal and the marriage ceremony together constitute lawful wedlock.

3. Of these the betrothal is held to be invalid, if a fault is discovered *in one of the parties;* and the essential characteristic of wifehood consists in the marriage benediction.

4. If *Brahmins, Kshatriyas, Vaiçyas* and *Çúdras* marry, wives of the same class should be preferred, and husbands of the same class for women of the same.

5. A *Brahmin* may take three wives of other classes in the order of classes; in the same way may a *Çúdra* woman take three husbands in the inverse order of classes.

6. The *Kshatriya* may marry two wives of other classes, the *Vaiçya* one; a *Vaiçya* woman may marry two other husbands, a *Kshatriya* woman one.

7. Marriages between persons belonging to the same family or kindred or race from the father's or mother's side are prohibited up to the seventh or fifth degree *of relationship.*

8. The men must be examined with regard to their

bodily qualities; if a man has no bodily defects, he may have the girl *of his choice.*

10. If a man has strong loins, knees, and bones, and if he is strong about the shoulders and the neck, if he has a broad back, and is born from the body (*tanuja*), and if his gait and voice are not feeble,

11. If his fæces, being thrown into water, swim *on the surface*, and if his seed and urine are foamy (?): one who possesses these characteristics is a man; otherwise, he is impotent.

12. Fourteen kinds of impotent persons have been mentioned in the law by the wise; they are either curable or incurable, as will be seen from the following enumeration.*

18. If a man is potent with another woman, but impotent with his own wife, she should take another husband, thus it has been ordained by *Prajápati.*

19. Women have been created for the sake of propagation, the woman is the field, the man the giver of the seed; the field must be given to him who has seed; he who has no seed must not possess it.

20. A father shall give his daughter in marriage himself, or a brother with the father's consent, or a grandfather, maternal uncle, kinsmen, or relatives;

21. In default of all these the mother, if she is

* The following curious, though highly indelicate, disquisition has been omitted, as most of the technical terms occurring in it are unintelligible and not met with in any other part of Sanskrit literature. Among the ancient Romans an analogous examination used to take place, in order to ascertain the disputed puberty of minors, who wanted to get rid of their tutors. Quinctilian mentions such an examination of the *habitus corporis* in a divorce case also; but the case he alludes to seems to be purely imaginary v. Savigny, "System des heut. röm. Rechts," iii, p. 56 foll.

qualified; if she is not, the remoter relations should give a girl in marriage.

22. If there be none of these, the girl shall apply to the king, and, having obtained his permission to make her own choice, choose a husband for herself,

23. Of the same class with her, and fitted for her in descent, qualities, age, and religious knowledge. Let her fulfil her duties jointly with, and procreate offspring, with him.

24. If a bridegroom goes abroad after the choice of his bride, she shall wait for his return for three seasons; afterwards let her choose another husband.

25. No girl should let the period of her maturity come on, without giving notice to her relations; if these *thereupon* do not give her in marriage to a husband, they are similar to murderers of embryos.

26. As many seasons pass by without her having a husband, so many times he who does not give her away, loads upon himself the crime of killing an embryo.

27. Therefore should a father give away his daughter for once *and all*, as soon as her menses appear, as great culpability would attach to him otherwise; this is the rule *established* among the virtuous.

28. Once is a share obtained at the partition of an inheritance, once is a girl given in marriage, and once does a man say, "I give:" these three are, by good men, done once for all *and irrevocably*.

29. This rule refers to the five *higher* kinds of marriage, beginning with the *Bráhma* marriage; in the three *lower* kinds, beginning with the *Ásura* marriage, the gift requires excellent qualities *in the bridegroom for its irrevocable validity*.

30. If a girl has been betrothed *by her father* in consideration of a marriage present, and a better bridegroom comes forward, who is endowed with religious, worldly, and amiable qualities, the *first* betrothal is null and void.

31. No man shall cast a blemish upon a faultless girl nor make a faultless man suspected; but if a blemish is discovered, it is no sin for them to separate.

32. If a man, having given a damsel in marriage in due form, does not deliver her to the bridegroom, he shall be punished by the king like a thief, in case the bridegroom be without defect.

33. But if a man gives a girl in marriage without indicating her blemish, the king shall inflict upon him the most rigid punishment.

34. If a man actuated by hatred says of a girl, "She is no maid," he is to be fined a hundred *panas* if he cannot prove her shame.

35. If a man abandons a girl without defects after he has chosen her, he is to be punished and must marry the girl even against his will.

36. To be afflicted with a long or disgraceful illness, deformed in limbs, to have lost her maidenhead, to be defiled, and to have lived with another man, these are the defects of a girl.

38. To be insane, an outcast, impotent, in a precarious condition, abandoned by his relations, and the two first defects of a girl, these are the blemishes of a bridegroom.

39. Eight forms of wedlock have been proclaimed for the marriages to be concluded by the *four* orders. The first of these is the *Bráhma,* the second the *Prájápatya* form.

40. Then come the *Ársha, Daiva, Gándharva,* and *Ásura* forms; the *Rákshasa* form is the seventh, and the *Paiçácha* the eighth.

41. By the *nuptial rite called Bráhma a father,* having decked his daughter with ornaments, gives her to a man whom he has invited and honourably received. The rite *Prájápatya* is *when the father gives away his daughter,* saying, "May both of you perform together your duties."

42. *When the father gives his daughter away,* after having received from the bridegroom clothes and a pair of kine, that marriage is termed *Ársha.* When he gives her to an officiating priest before the altar it is termed *Daiva.*

43. When a man and a woman unite from mutual desire, it is the fifth *form of marriage,* called *Gándharva.* The rite called *Ásura* is when the bride is given away in consideration of a nuptial present.

44. The seizure of a maiden by force is the marriage named *Rákshasa.* When the lover embraces a damsel in her sleep or one intoxicated, that marriage, the eighth and basest, is termed *Paiçácha.*

45. The four *first* of these *marriages,* the *Bráhma* and so forth, are declared to be legitimate; the *Gándharva marriage* is also *approved;* but the three remaining *marriages* are illegitimate.

46. Others are women who had a different husband before (*parapúrvá*); they are declared to be of seven kinds, in order *as enumerated:* among these, the twice-married woman is of three descriptions, and the disloyal wife of four sorts.

47. A damsel, not deflowered, but blemished by a *previous* marriage, is the first twice-married woman

(*punarbhú*); she must go through the marriage ceremony a second time.

48. She who deserts an infant husband, and has recourse to another man, but returns to the house of her husband, is considered as the second.

49. She who is given by her parents to a *Sapiṇḍa* of equal class, on failure of brothers-in-law, is considered as the third.

50. Whether she have borne children or be childless, a woman who, during her husband's life, unites herself to another man from carnal desire, is the first disloyal wife (*svairiṇí*).

51. She who, after the death of her husband, leaves her brother-in-law or other kinsman, with whom she has been living, and has connexion with a stranger through carnal desire, is considered as the second.

52. She who gives herself to another man, saying "I am thine," having come from *a different* country, or being purchased with money, or oppressed with hunger or thirst, is considered as the third.

53. She who has been given in marriage by her spiritual parents, *duly* considering the local usages, but through love accedes to another man, is also considered as a disloyal wife.

54. This rule is propounded in regard to twice-married and disloyal women; the first respectively *are more* despicable *than those subsequently mentioned;* and the last in order are preferable to those who precede them.

55. Their offspring belongs to the begetter, if they have come under his dominion in consideration of a price he has paid *to the husband;* but the children of ono who has not been sold, belongs to her husband.

56. If seed is strown upon a field without the owner's knowledge, the giver of the seed has no *right to a* share in the crop, and the produce belongs to the owner of the field.

57. If seed is carried away by wind or water into *a* field, and germinates there, the plant belongs to the landowner, the *mere* sower takes not the fruit.

58. If a bull begets calves while being on the pasture ground of a stranger, they belong to him who owns the calves, and the seed of the bull has been wasted.

59. If seed is strown upon a field with the owner's permission, it is considered as belonging both to the owner of the seed and to the proprietor of the soil.

60. Soil would not *be productive* without seed, nor is seed productive without soil; therefore offspring is by right the joint property of the father and mother.

61. Again there is no *legitimate* issue *produced*, if a man has had intercourse with a woman in the house of another man; and it is termed fornication by the learned if a woman has intercourse with a man in the house of a stranger.

62. Sexual intercourse with other men's wives is not criminal, if *the wronged husband* is an offender, or if he has abandoned his wife, or if he is impotent or consumptive.

63. To meet with others' wives in unseasonable [solitary] places, and at unseasonable hours, and to sit, speak, and amuse one's self with them, are the three gradations of adultery.

64. The meeting of a man and a woman at the junction of two rivers, at a place of pilgrimage, in gardens or parks, is also called an adulterous act.

65. By the sending of messengers and exchange of letters, and various other criminal acts of this kind adultery may be known by the wise.

66. If a man touches a woman *on her breasts, or* any *other* place which ought not to be touched, or, being touched *unbecomingly* by her, bears it complacently, all such acts, committed with mutual consent, are termed adulterous proceedings.

67. If a man takes hold of a woman's hand, hair, or the border of her gown, or exclaims, "stop, stop," to her, this is also called an adulterous proceeding.

68. Adultery may be known by the wise by the sending of clothes, ornaments, garlands, drinks, eatbles, and fragrant articles.

69. If a man himself declares from vanity, ignorance, or vain-glory, "I once embraced this or that woman," it is also called an adulterous act.

70. For adultery committed with a woman of the same class, the highest amercement should be inflicted; if it has been committed with a person of any inferior class, the middling amercement; for adultery with a person of any superior class, capital punishment.

71. For touching the private parts of an unmarried woman with two fingers against her will, death and confiscation of the whole property is ordained.

72. If a man has intercourse with an unmarried woman, who consents to it, it is no offence, but he shall deck her with ornaments, worship her, and thus bring her to his house as his bride.

73. One who has criminal connexion with any of these *twenty-one descriptions of women,* viz., mother, mother's sister, mother-in-law, maternal uncle's wife,

father's sister, paternal uncle's wife, friend's wife, pupil's wife, sister, sister's friend, daughter-in-law,

74. Daughter, spiritual guide's wife, a woman of the same lineage, a woman dependent on his protection, the queen, a female ascetic, a nurse, a well-behaved woman, and a *Bráhmaṇí*,

75. Is said to be as guilty as the violator of his religious preceptor's bed. For such a crime as this there is no other penalty short of the excision of the male organ.

76. If a man has unnatural intercourse with animals he shall be fined ten hundred *paṇas*; if with a cow, he shall be fined 500 *paṇas*; the latter fine shall also be inflicted upon a man who has connexion with a woman of the lowest class.

77. If a man has connexion with a woman with whom intercourse is forbidden, the king shall inflict punishment upon him; but in order to atone for the sin committed he must do penance.

78. A man may have intercourse with any woman, not a *Bráhmaṇí*, who is disloyal to her husband, a prostitute, a female slave not shut up by her master*, *and, in general,* with women of a lower order than his own, but not with women of a higher order.

79. But among these, sexual intercourse with females who are kept by another, is as criminal as adultery with another man's wife; and intercourse with common

* According to the Mitákshará. Another, far less plausible, explanation of the term *nishkásiní* is quoted in the Víramitrodaya, 510, and seems to have been followed by Borrodaile, May. xix, 11.

prostitutes is likewise forbidden, if they are in the service of another man.

80. If the husband of a childless woman dies, she shall approach her brother-in-law, through a wish that male issue should be obtained, being authorized to do so by her spiritual parents.

81. And he may approach her until a son has been born to them. When a son is begotten he must refrain; since an incest would be *committed* otherwise.

82. Having anointed his limbs with clarified butter, or with expressed oil, averting his face from hers, and shunning the contact of limb with limb,

83. A younger *or an elder* brother, authorized by spiritual parents, may approach his brother's wife; for it is done in order that the family may be perpetuated, for the sake of offspring, and not through amorous desire.

84. *He may approach* a woman who has had children, and who is respectable, and free from lust and passion; but he must not approach one who is with child, immoral, or unauthorized by her relations.

85. If a woman should bear a son to her brother-in-law, without being authorized by her relations, he is considered a bastard and incapable of inheriting by those who know the Veda.

86. And if a younger brother should approach, without authorization, the wife of his elder brother, or an elder brother the wife of his younger brother, they are both as guilty as the violator of his religious preceptor's bed.

87. Let him inform and approach her, being directed

by his spiritual parents, once, or until she be pregnant, according to the abovementioned rule.

88. But if the man or woman act otherwise, through carnal desire, they shall both receive severe punishment from the king; else justice is violated.

89. Man and wife should not quarrel before either their relations or the king, on account of a dispute sprung from jealousy or passion.

90. It is a crime in them both if man and wife forsake each other, or if they persist in mutual dislike, except in the case of adultery of a guarded wife.

91. If a woman commit adultery, tonsure, a low couch, mean food, a miserable habitation, and the task of removing ordures, *constitute her punishment.*

92. A woman who embezzles all *her husband's* wealth under pretence of female property, or who procures abortion, or who wishes the death of her husband, shall be banished from the town.

93. Let *a man* speedily banish from his house a wife who constantly dissipates wealth, and her who speaks unkindly, and who eats before her husband.

94. Let him not dignify with his love a barren wife, nor one who only bears daughters, nor one who deserves blame, nor one who is constantly at variance with him; if he does, he partakes of her faults.

95. A man who forsakes his wife, although being submissive, not harsh in her speeches, skilful, chaste, and fertile, should be brought back to his duty by the king with a severe punishment.

96. If an unblemished girl has been married to a man who has a secret blemish, and has not gone to another man *after discovering it,* she shall be enjoined to do so by her relations; if she has none, she may do so of her own accord.

97. There are five cases in which a woman may take another husband: her *first* husband having perished, or died *naturally*, or gone abroad, or if he be impotent, or have lost his caste.

98. Let a *Brahmin* woman wait eight years for her absent husband, or else, if she be childless, four years, and then betake herself to another man.

99. A *Kshatriya* woman should wait for six years, or, if she be childless, for three years; a *Vaiçya* woman should wait for four years if she has children, if not, for two years.

100. The same period is not prescribed for *Çúdra* women whose husbands are absent; the double period *is ordained* in case the husband is understood to be alive.

101. This law has been ordained by *Prajápati* for women whose husbands do not return; it is not considered as a crime if they approach another man after *the above period.*

102. This rule has been propounded for those who are born of women of *the same or* a lower class than their husbands; those born of women of a higher class than their husbands are said to have sprung from a *sinful* mixture of classes.

103. There are sons begotten in the direct order of classes, without an interval, or with one *class,* or with two *classes, between those of their parents, or Anantaras, Ekántaras,* and *Dvyantaras,* and the same *distinction is observed among sons begotten* in an inverse order.*

* The following enumeration of the mixed castes is neither complete nor very systematical. This may be owing to a corruption of the text, since two half-Çlokas at least of the MSS. are manifest interpolations and had to be rejected. See Appendix.

104. *This is the origin of* the *Ugra*, the *Páráçava*, and the *Nish áda*, *who are begotten* in the direct order; of the *Ambashṭha*, *Mágadha*, and *Ksháttṛi*, who is the son of a *Kshatriya* woman.

105. Of these, one is born in the direct order, and two are born in an inverse order: the *Kshattṛi* and the like are born in an inverse, those mentioned before him, in the direct order.

106. The son of *a Brahmin by a Brahmin* woman is of the same class *with his father*, a son of the same with a woman of the *Kshatriya* class is an *Anantara*. *The Ambashṭha* is an *Ekántara*, *namely*, the son of a *Brahmin* with a *Vaiçya* woman.

107. In the same manner, a class called *Nisháda* springs from the union of a *Kshatriya* with a *Çúdra* woman. A *Çúdra* woman procreates a better son, called *Páráçava*, with a *Brahmin*.

108. Thus the sons born in the direct order have been enumerated. The *Súta*, the *Mágadha*, and the *Áyogava*, as well as the *Kshattri* and the *Vaidehaka*, are mentioned

109. As the sons born in the inverse order of the *four* classes. A *Súta* is considered as an *Anantara*, being begotten by a *Kshatriya* on a *Brahmin* wife.

110. The *Mágadha* and *Áyogava* are likewise *Anantaras*, springing from a *Vaiçya* and a *Çúdra* father *respectively*. A *Bráhmaṇí* wife bears to a *Vaiçya* an *Ekántara*, called *Vaidehaka*.

111. A *Kshatriya* wife bears to a *Çúdra* a son, *called Kshattṛi*, who is an *Ekántara*. A *Dvyantara* in the inverse order of classes, the basest *of mortals*, of sinful origin, is born from a *Çúdra* by a *Bráhmáṇí*, if she

forgets herself *so far as to have connexion with a such.*

112. Therefore let the king take special care to restrain the women from sinful intercourse with men of other classes than their own.

---

## XIII. Head of Dispute.

### *Partition of Heritage.*

1. Where a distribution of the paternal estate is instituted by sons, it is called by the wise Partition of Heritage, a head of dispute.

2. After the father's death let sons divide his estate according to the order *of their seniority and caste; let* daughters *divide the estate* of their mother *after her death, or*, in default of daughters, their issue.

3. *Or let them divide the estate* when the mother's menses have ceased, and the sisters have been married, or when cohabitation has ceased, and the father's carnal desire is extinguished.

4. Or the father, being advanced in years, may himself institute the division among his sons; either *dismissing* the eldest with the best share, or however *else* his inclination may prompt him.

5. Or let the eldest brother support the rest like a father, if they consent *to live together*; or even the youngest brother, if he is capable to do so: the prosperity of a family depends upon ability.

6. But what is gained by valour, and the property

of a wife, and what is acquired by science, these three *sorts of property* must not be divided; and any favour conferred by the father is likewise *exempt from partition.*

7. And if the mother has given through affection *a portion of* her property to one of her sons, the above rule refers to that also; for the mother is like the father *competent to bestow gifts.*

8. What was given before the nuptial fire, what was presented in the bridal procession, her husband's donation, and what has been given by her brother, mother, or father, is termed the sixfold property of a woman.

9. This *separate* property of women is declared to go to their issue, but, if they are childless, to their husbands, in case *they were married according to one* of the four *higher* rites, the first of which is the *Bráhma* rite; and to the parents, in case *they were married according to one* of the other *rites.**

10. He who maintains the family of a brother studying science, shall take a portion of the wealth gained by science, though he be ignorant himself.†

11. A learned man needs not give a share of his own acquired wealth, without his assent, to an unlearned co-heir: provided it were not gained by him using the paternal estate.

* See for the eight rites of marriage above, 12, 39 ff.

† According to Tagore's (Viv.) version of this Çloka, a brother would acquire this right only when he supports his brother's family *during his absence from home* to acquire learning, a restriction neither contained in the words of the text, nor supported by Colebrooke's and Burnell's (Dáyavibh.) translations of this passage. See also Goldstücker "On the deficiencies," etc , p. 8.

12. Let the father making a partition reserve two shares for himself; the mother shall receive an equal share with the sons, *if they divide* after her husband's death.

13. The eldest shall receive a larger share *upon partition after the father's death,* and for the youngest a smaller one is declared. The rest should take equal shares, and so should an unmarried sister.

14. For sons of the wife lawfully begotten upon her, the same *rule is ordained;* for those who are of an inferior caste, born of women legally married, a decrease in the shares according to their order is ordained.

15. For such as have been separated by their father with an equal, greater, or less allotment of wealth, that is a lawful distribution; for the father is the lord of all.

16. A father who is afflicted with disease, or influenced by wrath, or whose mind is engaged by a beloved object, or who acts otherwise than the law permits, has no power in the distribution of the estate.

17. The son of a damsel, the son of a pregnant bride, and he who was born of a woman who was *at first* unknown, *but found out afterwards*: the husband *of their mothers* is the father of these, and they receive shares *of his property.*

18. Let the damsel's son, born through his mother's folly, whose father is unknown, present the funeral cake to the father of his mother and inherit his property.

19. But those children who have been begotten on a wife not appointed, by one or by many, receive no share; they are the sons of the begetter.

20. Let them present the funeral cake to their begetter, if their mother had been obtained *from her husband* in consideration of a present; but if they were born of a woman obtained without a present, they present the funeral cake to the husband *of their mother*.

21. An enemy to his father, an outcast, an impotent person, and one formally expelled from society, take no shares of the inheritance, even though they be legitimate: much less, if they be the sons of the wife by an appointed kinsman.

22. *Incapable of inheriting are also* persons afflicted with a chronic or an agonizing disease, idiots, madmen, and lame men; and these must be maintained by the family; but their sons take their respective shares.

23. Let sons of two fathers present the funeral cakes and the oblations of water to both severally; let them take half a share respectively of the inheritance of their begetter, and of their mother's husband.

24. The share of reunited *brothers* is considered to be exclusively theirs; otherwise, *i.e. on failure of reunited brothers*, they cannot take the inheritance; it shall go to other *brothers*, when no issue is left.*

25. Amongst brothers, if any one die without issue, or enter a religious order, let the rest of the brothers divide his wealth, except the wife's separate property.

* Translated according to the third of the explanations of this difficult passage propounded in Colebrooke's Digest v, 8, ccccxxxiii. For Bühler's different rendering of it, see his D. p. 354, who thinks that Colebrooke had another reading of this passage before him than Balambhaṭṭa's, v. Appendix.

26. Let them allow a maintenance to his women for life, provided these preserve unsullied the bed of their lord. But, if they behave otherwise, the brethren may resume that allowance.

27. *As regards* the daughter of a deceased *coparcener*, her maintenance shall be made out of her father's share; let them support her until her marriage, afterwards her husband shall keep her.

28. After the death of the husband, his kin are the guardians of a childless widow; in disposing *of her*, and in the care of her, as well as in her maintenance, they have full power.

29. But if the husband's family be extinct, or contain no male, or be helpless, the kin of her own father are the guardians of the widow, if there be no relations within the degree of a *Sapiṇḍa*.

30. Through independence women go to ruin, though they be born in *a noble* family; therefore the Lord of Creatures ordained dependence for them.

31. The father protects her during her childhood, her husband in her youth, her sons in her old age; a woman has no right to independence.

32. What remains of the paternal inheritance over and above the father's obligations, and after payment of his debts, may be divided by the brethren; so that their father continue not a debtor.

33. For those whose forms of initiation have not been regularly performed by the father, these ceremonies must be completed by the brethren out of the patrimony.

34. If no wealth of the father exist, the ceremonies must be, without fail, defrayed by brothers already initiated, contributing funds out of their own portions.

35. But he who, being employed in the affairs of the family, performs their business, must be honoured by his brethren by *presents of* food, dress, and vehicles.

36. If a question arise among co-heirs in regard to the fact of partition, it must be ascertained by *the evidence of* kinsmen, by the record of the distribution, or by the separate transaction of affairs.

37. The religious duty of unseparated brethren is single. When partition indeed has been made, religious duties become separate for each of them.

38. Gift, and acceptance of gift, cattle, grain, houses, land, and attendants must be considered as distinct among separate brethren, as also diet, religious duties, income, and expenditure.*

39. Separated, not unseparated, brethren may reciprocally bear testimony, become sureties, bestow gifts, and accept presents.

40. Those by whom such matters are publicly transacted with their co-heirs, may be known to be separate, even without written evidence.

41. Those brothers who live for ten years, performing their religious duties, and carrying on their transactions, separately, ought to be considered separate; that is certain.

42. When there are many descended from one, who perform their religious duties, and carry on their transactions, separately, and possess separate materials

* Colebrooke, in his version of this Çloka, Dig. v, 6, ccclxxx, and ibid.ccclxxxvii, (but not Dáy. xiv, 7, where it is also quoted), adds: "and *conversely* as signs of partition;" but these words are not contained in the Sanskrit text.

for their work, if such persons not being accordant in affairs,

43. Should give or sell their shares, they may do all that as they please: for they are masters of their own wealth.*

44. A son born after division shall alone take the paternal wealth; or he shall participate with the coparcener reunited *with his father.*

45. The legitimate son, the son begotten on a wife, the son of an appointed daughter, a damsel's son, the son of a pregnant bride, the son born secretly,

46. The son of a twice-married woman, the son cast off, the son obtained *through adoption,* the son bought, the son made, and the self-given son, are declared to be the twelve *kinds of* sons.

47. Six of these are kinsmen and heirs, and six are kinsmen, but not heirs; it is recorded that each preceding one is of higher rank, and each following one of lower rank.

48. If a doubt arise as to the ownership of a house or field, whose possession has been interrupted, *the claimant* shall obtain it by *producing* records, or persons who knew him to be possessed of it, or witnesses.†

49. After the father's death *the above-mentioned sons*

* The translation of this passage agrees with Borrodaile's May. iv, 7, 36, and differs slightly from Bühler's, and more strongly from Colebrooke's version, v, 7, cccxc.

† This verse, though found in all the MSS., is clearly an interpolation, as already Bühler has hinted. In Colebrooke's Dig. v, 4, clxxxviii, where the whole of the above passage is quoted, 47 is immediately followed by 49.

succeed to his wealth in their order; on failure of the superior, let the inferior in order take the heritage.

50. On failure of the son, the daughter inherits; for she equally continues the lineage. A son and a daughter both continue the race of their father.

51. On failure of daughters, the nearer kin inherit, next the remoter relations, next a fellow-caste man; on failure of all, the heritage goes to the king,

52. Except in the case of *Brahmins*; but a king, attentive to his duty, shall allot a maintenance to the wives of the deceased. This is declared to be the law of inheritance.

---

## XIV. Head of Dispute.

### *Violence.*

1. Violence (*sáhasa*) means whatever act is by strength performed by persons inflamed with power; for strength (*sahas, whence sáhasa*) is *also* termed power (*bala*).

2. Manslaughter, theft, the handling of another man's wife, and insult, with its two subdivisions, are the four kinds of violence.

3. It is again divided into three sorts in the law-books, *viz.*, violence of the first, middle, and third degree, the characteristics of each being as follows:

4. Spoiling fruits, roots, water, and such things, and agricultural implements, or throwing them away,

treading them under foot, or the like, is declared to be violence of the first degree.

5. *Injuring* in the same way clothes, cattle, food, drink, and household articles, is declared to be violence of the middle *degree.*

6. Malicious practices with poison, weapons, and the like, the handling of another man's wife, and all other offences directed against the life *of a human being,* are called violence of the highest degree.

7. The punishment for violence must be in proportion to the crime; *but,* in the first degree, not less than one hundred *paṇas; the penalty* for violence of the second degree is fixed by those acquainted with the law at not less than five hundred *paṇas.*

8. Execution, confiscation of the whole property, banishment from the town, branding, and amputation of the limbs with which a crime has been committed, are the punishments declared for violence of the highest degree.

9. This measure of punishment is laid down for all without distinction of class,* only *the punishment* of *Brahmins* must be short of execution.

10. Shaving of the head, banishment from the town, a mark on the forehead indicating his crime, and parading him upon an ass, shall be his punishment.

11. *Those who have committed a crime* of the two first degrees may be admitted into society, after having received their punishment; but one guilty of

* Borrodaile, May. xviii, 6, wrongly: "From there being no difference [in the degrees of guilt] the same measure of punishment is laid down for all."

violence of the highest degree must not be spoken to, even though he have atoned for his crime.

12. Theft is one of the elements of it [of violence], but there is this difference between both, that violence signifies injury done *to others by strength,* theft the same done by fraud.

13. Theft is again declared by the wise to be of three sorts according to the *value of the stolen* goods, since articles of inferior, middling, and superior value may be stolen.

14. Earthenware utensils, camphor, a stool, a bedstead, *articles made of* bone, wood, leather, grass and the like, leguminous grains, and boiled rice, are termed inferior articles.

15. Clothes, *made of any material* except silk, and similarly cattle *of every description* except kine, *all* metals except gold, as well as rice and barley, are termed articles of middling value.

16. Gold, jewels, silk, women, men, kine, elephants, horses, and the property of the gods, of *Brahmins,* and the king, are the articles of superior value.

17. To injure in any way the property of others, while they are asleep or take no notice or are intoxicated, is named theft by the wise.

18. Theft is proved against a man who is caught with the stolen goods; the possession of the stolen goods *is proved against those* who are seen to enjoy them; suspicion *arises* if a man frequents bad society, and makes extraordinary expenses.

19. They who grant food and shelter to thieves, who seek their protection, and they who wink *at their escape,* though able *to stop them,* are accomplices in their offence.

20. Those, who though being within hearing, do not render assistance to people who call for help, while *robbers* are taking away their property, are also accomplices of the crime.

21. The *three kinds of* penalties which the sages have fixed for the three degrees of violence, are also applicable in case of theft according to the *above-mentioned* gradation of articles *liable to be stolen.*

22. If cows or the like have been lost, or any kind of property has been taken away, let experienced men trace out the thief's footmarks.

23. Wherever the trace goes, be it to a village or a pasture ground or a solitude, that district has to make good that which may have been stolen, if the footmark be not carried forward *from that district.*

24. If the trace be obscured, or interrupted by a pit, or by the footmarks of other people, the village or pasture district nearest to it shall be made to pay for the loss.

25. If the *footmarks* of two men are found upon one road, he is in most cases the offender who has stood charged with other crimes before, or who mingles with bad society. (? See Appendix.)

26. Let *Chandálas,* murderers, and the like, and those who live at night, make inquiry after the malefactors in villages, and let those who live in the country *make a search for them* in the country..

27. If the thieves are not caught, let the king make good what has been stolen, from his own purse; if he is indulgent towards criminals, justice and *his own* interest is violated.

## XV. (and XVI.) Head of Dispute.

### *Abuse and Assault.*

1. Reviling in vehement and abusive terms a person's country, class, race, and so forth, is named Abuse.

2. It is of three kinds, namely, *nishṭhur, açlíla,* and *tibra*; the difference of the punishment varies as the nature of the abuse.

3. *Nishṭhur* is equivalent to abusive language; *Açlíla* is insulting language couched in vehement terms; *Tibra* is the charging with a mortal sin.

4. Injury inflicted upon the limbs of another, with the hand, foot, weapons, and so forth, and defiling him with ashes and the like, is named Assault.

5. Here again there is a threefold division, since an Assault may be of the *first or* moderate, of the middle, and of the gravest kind, according as it consisted in menacingly uplifting *a hand or weapon only,* or in a sudden attack, or in the laying open a sore.

6. Even so there are three degrees in every act of robbery, according as articles of inferior, middling, or superior value are stolen; the offenders shall be punished.

7 Again, five cases are said *to be possible* in both *abuse and assault,* if the respective innocence or culpability of the two parties is inquired into.

8. If no difference is observable in the respective guilt of two persons, who stand both charged with the

crime of abuse or assault, their punishment shall be equal.

9. He from whom the first attack has proceeded deserves special blame; he who returns it is likewise criminal; but it is the first aggressor upon whom the heavier punishment falls.

10. If both parties have suffered equally, the punishment falls upon him who begins afresh *to attack his adversary,* whether he was *originally* the first aggressor or not.

11. If a public executioner, a *Meda,* a *Chandála,* a deformed person, a killer *of animals,* a groom of elephants, a *Vrátya,* or a slave, insult persons commanding respect, or teachers, or trespass upon the ground *of a stranger,*

12. He shall be punished immediately *according to his guilt;* and the legislators do not look upon violence committed against such persons as a wrong.

13. If any of those low persons has offended his superior, the latter shall punish him *in person,* and the king shall not amerce them in a fine.

14. For these are the dregs of society, and their property, too, is like dregs; the king also shall inflict corporal punishment upon, but not fine, them.

15. A *Kshatriya* who insults a *Brahmin* shall be fined a hundred *paṇas;* a *Vaiçya,* one hundred and a half, or two hundred; but a *Çúdra* shall be executed.

16. A *Brahmin* shall be fined fifty *paṇas* for reviling a *Kshatriya;* the fine for a *Vaiçya* shall be the half of fifty, *or twenty-five;* and for a *Çúdra,* twelve *paṇas.*

17. It shall be twelve *paṇas* in case of an insult of a member of a twice-born class against a man of his own class; this amount shall be doubled if *the*

*abuse was couched* in words which ought not to be uttered.

18. If a man taxes another with being blind with one eye, or lame, or defective in any similar way, he shall be fined by the king not less than a *kárshápaṇa*, even though he speak truth.

19. One must not upbraid a man with a crime which he has atoned for as prescribed by law, or for which he has been *duly* punished by the king; by trespassing against this rule one becomes liable to punishment.

20. Two beings are declared to be in this world that must neither be blamed nor chastised, a *Brahmin* and a king; for these two are the bearers of the world.

21. A man calling a degraded man fallen, or taxing a thief with being such, is as great a sinner *as those persons*, if his reproof is just; * if it is unjust, he obtains double blame.

22. If a once-born man use bad language against members of the twice-born classes, his tongue shall be cut off; for he is of base origin.

23. But if he attacks their name or race in abusive terms, an iron style, of the length of ten fingers, shall be thrust red-hot into his mouth.

24. If, through pride, he gives religious instruction to twice-born men, the king shall order hot oil to be dropped into his mouth and ears.

25. With whatever limb a low-born man hurt a *Brahmin*, that limb of his shall be cut off; thus his crime will be atoned for.

26. If an inferior desires to sit on the same seat with

* *vacanát tulya-doshaḥ syát*. Borrodaile, May. xvi, 1, 6, translates (A man taxing a thief with being such) *commits no fault* (sic).

his superior, he shall be banished, after having his hinder parts stamped, or he shall be deprived of his buttock.

27. If he spit on his superior, through pride, the king shall cause his lips to be cut off; if he urine *on his superior,* his penis; if he break wind *on him,* his anus.

28. If he seize *his superior* by the hair, feet, beard, back, or testicles, the king shall cut off his hands without hesitation.

29. If the skin be torn off, and blood be produced, *the aggressor* shall be fined a hundred *paṇas;* six *nishkas,* if the flesh be visible; and he shall be banished, if he break a bone.

30. He who defames a king persistent in the discharge of his duties, shall atone for his offence by having his tongue cut off and all his property confiscated.

31. The sinner who beats even a guilty king shall be impaled, and burnt alive, since he is worse than a murderer of a hundred *Brahmins.*

32. A father is not punishable for his son's crimes, nor is the owner of a horse, dog, or ape *responsible for any damage they may have done,* unless he have caused them to do it.

## XVI. (XVII.) Head of Dispute.

### *Gambling with Dice and Living Creatures.*

1. False gambling with dice, pieces of leather, and little staves, *made of ivory*, and the like,* as well as betting on birds, are comprised under the head of dispute termed Gambling with Dice and Living Creatures.

2. Let the master of the gaming-house conduct the game, and enforce payment of the stake which has been fixed [*or, with a change of the subject of the sentence*, and let the gambler pay his stake]. The share of the master of the gaming-house shall amount to ten per cent.

3. If in a game the *adversary's* dice show the double number in falling, the victory is his, and the gambler loses *his stake*; thus say those conversant with gambling at dice.

4. In quarrels among gamblers, let other gamblers be consulted; they shall decide them, and bear testimony in them.

5. Let no gamester enter another gaming-house without having first settled his account; nor must he refuse *to pay his due* to the master of the gaming-house; on the contrary, he must pay it of his own accord.

6. The wicked men who make use of false dice shall be expelled from the gaming-house, after having a

* Translated according to the Mit. and Vír. ad h. l.

wreath of dice hung round their neck; for this is the punishment ordained for them.

7. He who gambles with dice without the king's permission, shall not get the stake of the game, nay he shall be fined.

8. Or let the gamester pay a share to the king to the above-mentioned amount, and play in public; thus the law will not be violated. *

---

## XVII. (XVIII.) Head of Dispute.

### *Miscellaneous Disputes.*

1. Under the head of Miscellaneous Disputes judicial matters connected with the sovereign are treated: they relate to the injunctions and prohibitions of kings, and to the duties they have to fulfil,

2. *And comprise* rules regarding towns,† an enumeration of the constituent elements of a state,‡ the

* This verse should be inserted immediately after 2, which is in fact followed by it in a quotation occurring in the Víramitrodaya, p. 718. Both verses belong together, stating the two restrictions under which a king allows his subjects to indulge their passion for gambling.

† *puraḥ pramáṇam,* Mitramiçra reads in quoting this passage in the Vír. The MSS. and the Mit. read *puraḥ pradánam,* "the gift or grant of a town," (to a younger prince of a royal family ?).

‡ Their traditional number is five, viz., the ministers, treasure, territory, fortresses, and army; to these are added the king himself and the sovereign who is his ally, Manu ix, 294.

body of laws for heretics, traders, companies *of merchants,* and assemblages *of kinsmen,*

3. Quarrels between father and son, penances and offences, receipt and abstraction *of goods,* and the wrath of anachorets,

4. Crimes connected with the mixture of classes, the substance and regulations prescribed for them; in short, whatever has not been treated in the former *heads of dispute,* shall be treated under *the head of* Miscellaneous *Disputes.*

5. A king shall keep a careful watch over all orders and over his subjects *in general,* with the four means indicated in the law-books.*

6. Having seen any order whatsoever swerve from the path of duty and failing to fulfil its duties or exceeding its proper limits, let him again bring it back to its path.

7. Likewise, if other sinful acts are committed that are not in keeping with the precepts of law, a king shall inflict punishment on the delinquents.

8. Let not the king do that which is inconsistent with law and usage, nor what is injurious to his subjects; if that, which is so, be practised, let him check *such conduct.*

9. If another king has done a wicked deed, contrary to justice, let him redress it, according to maxims ordained by traditional law.

10. The weapons of soldiers, the tools of tradespeople, the ornaments of professional prostitutes, musical instruments of those who make a profession of playing them,

* They are, according to Manu 7, 107, *negotiation, presents, division, and force of arms.*

11. And any implements by which working people gain their substance, must not be seized by the king, even when he confiscates their entire property.

12. A king and a *Brahmin* must not be admonished nor reprimanded, on account of their majesty and sanctity, unless they have swerved from the path *of duty*.

13. The unrighteous man, who does not obey the laws promulgated by the king, shall be punished and *even* put to death for infringement of the king's commandments.

14. If the king did not inflict punishment *on the evil-doers* of any class whatsoever who have deviated from the path *of duty, all* the living beings would perish;

15. The *Brahmin* would forsake *his brother Brahmin*, the *Kshatriya his brother Kshatriya*, and the stronger would devour the weaker like fish on a spit.

16. The *Vaiçya* would give up his work, and the *Çúdra* engross everything, if the kings did not inflict punishment on their subjects.

17. To be the stronghold of the righteous, and the terror of the unrighteous, this is held to be the duty of kings; it is their interest to oppress their enemies.

18. As fire is not soiled though it be constantly burning living beings, even so a king does not stain himself *with guilt*, who inflicts punishment on those who deserve it.

19. Wisdom is the ornament of kings; it shows itself in their sayings; *but* whatever *sentence* they pronounce, right or wrong, is the law for litigants.

20. *Law* lives upon the earth visibly in shape of the

king, with a thousand eyes; men can never prosper if they infringe his commandments.

21. Whatever a king does for the protection of his subjects, by right of his kingly power, and for the best of mankind, is valid; that is the rule.

22. As a husband should always be respected by his wives, even though he be a feeble man, a monarch should always be respected by his subjects, even though he be a bad ruler.

23. The king's sentence decides disputes, in order that the subjects fearing his edicts may not deviate from the path *of duty*.

24. The rulers of the earth have made regulations for the purpose of maintaining order; the king's sentence is even more weighty than these regulations.

25. It is through devotion that kings have acquired dominion over their subjects; therefore kings are absolute rulers: the subjects of a king must obey his commandments, and they derive their substance from him.

26. The kings, endowed with immense power, take five *different* shapes, that of *Agni*, of *Indra*, of *Soma*, of *Yama*, and of the God of Wealth.

27. A monarch is termed *Agni* [fire] if, having got angry with or without reason, he burns [torments] his subjects.

28. A king is termed *Indra*, if relying upon his power he attacks his enemies with uplifted weapon, desirous of conquering them.

29. A king is termed *Soma*, if, giving up his burning wrath, he presents himself to his subjects with a cheerful face.

30. He is termed *Vaivasvata* (*Yama*) if, having

majestically placed himself on the throne of judgment, he dictates punishments *and deals* even-handed justice towards all his subjects.

31. He is termed the God of Wealth if he gratifies with presents the distressed, reverend persons, wise men, servants, and the like.

32. Therefore you must not disregard him, nor stir his wrath, nor displease him, and you must obey his orders; destruction *would wait upon you*, were you to infringe them.

33. His duties consist in protecting his subjects, honouring the old and wise, examining law-suits, and keeping *each order* in its due bounds.

34. A king shall always be careful to pay regard to the *Brahmins;* he shall appear before them the first thing in the morning and salute them all.

35. When he meets *one of* the seven or nine *virtuous mendicants*, another man must make way to pass by for him (? Manu 11, 1).* Such *Brahmins* may freely enter the houses of strangers, in order to collect alms.

36. They shall take or receive fire-wood, flowers, and water, without *its being considered* theft, and talk to the wives of others without fear of other men.

37. They shall have to pay no fares in crossing rivers, and be conveyed across them before *other people*, but they shall have to pay fares and tolls in trading.

38. A travelling *Brahmin*, being tired and having no food, does not commit an offence by taking two canes of sugar and two roots *from a stranger's field.*

* See Appendix.

39. *Brahmins must* not *take alms* from those accused *of a crime,* nor from outcasts, nor from their adversaries, nor from atheists, nor from persons in distress, nor from a spendthrift, nor by force.

40. They may take alms from rich people on account of their riches, and from generous people on account of their liberality; from kings, *and, generally speaking,* from everybody, except from *other* Brahmins.

41. There is no difference between a dutiful king and a *Brahmin,* who both truly protect mankind.

42. Even a severe ruler's wealth is considered pure, if he knows his duty, possesses wisdom and punishes the unrighteous in order to protect *his realm.*

43. He who accepts presents from a wicked king, whose conduct is not in keeping with the precepts of the Law, *will have to* pass through the twenty-one hells successively.

44. The income of kings is comparable to the conflux of clean and unclean floods, which mingle in the ocean.

45. As tin becomes clean when it is brought into a blazing fire, wealth acquired by whatever means becomes clean in the hands of a king.

46. Whoever gives his property away to *Brahmins,* must have a special permission to do so from the king; this is an eternal law.

47. Both the sixth part of what is acquired in some other customary way, and *the sixth part of the produce of* the land, is *the king's* due, the reward *obtained by him* for the protection of his subjects.

48. He may take away again what he has given, if it was not a grant made to *Brahmins;* but what has been given to *Brahmins,* may never be taken back *by him.*

49. To give, to read, and to make offerings, are his [*the Brahmin's*] three duties; to perform sacrifices *for others*, to teach, and to receive presents, are his three modes of livelihood.

50. The *Brahmin* shall fulfil his duties, receive his substance from the king, and not accept presents from *persons belonging to* vile castes, if there is piety in him.

51. Is not a king a god, since it is his word which makes dishonest men honest, and, on the other hand, honest men dishonest?

52. Those who, knowing the divine nature of a king endowed with infinite majesty, accept presents from him, are by no means defiled *by them*.

53. There are eight things to be reverenced in this world: a *Brahmin*, a cow, fire, gold, butter, the *Ádityas*, the floods, and, lastly, a king.

54. You must always regard, honour, and worship these, and pay reverence to them, in order to prolong your existence.

# APPENDIX,

containing an index of the quotations from this work in some of the principal Dharmanibandhas or Digests, and of the parallel passages found in the code of Manu; and critical notes.

For an explanation of the abbreviations used in this Appendix, see pp. xxiii, xxix, xxx.

---

Introduction. 1. *veda-vedáṅga-yajna-vidhána-chámáro*, MSS. I have supplied *adhyayana* after *vedáṅga* and altered *chámáro* into (*vidhána*) *mácháro*.

1.

2, 3a.—Vír. 5 (with several different readings). 5.—Vír. 6. 7.—Ragh. 13. Vír. 71, 117. 8.—Colebrooke "On Hindu Courts of Justice." Essays (London, 1873) i, 503. 9–25.—Vír. 7, with slight discrepancies in the order of the several Çlokas and in the choice of expressions. 16.—Col. Ess. i, 509. 21.—Mit. 7. 23.—Mit. 7. 25a.—Mit. 32.* 25b.—Ragh. 15. 31.—Mit. 5. Col. Ess. i, 511. 34.—Ragh. 53. May. i, 12. *35a.—Vír. 119. *37.—Vír.

125. 38.—Ragh. 16. 40.—Vír. 139. 42.—Vír. 102. *43, 44.—Mit. 9. Vír. 55. May. i, 16. 45.—May. ibid. 45–48.—Mit. 9. *45–49.—Vír. 53, 55, 56. 47–49.—Ragh. 7, 8. 55, 56.—Vír. 108. Mit. 110. 55.—May iii, 2, 21. 58.—Ragh. 62. Mit. 359. *59. —Vír. 123. 61.—Ragh. 15. Col. Ess. i, 519. 65–68.—Col. Ess. i, 519. 520. 68.—Vir. 125.

Between 24 and 25 the following Çloka is inserted in both MSS.: *suniçchitabaládánas* (sic) *tv arthí* (L *athí*) *svártha-prachoditaḥ* (for *prachoditam?*) || *lekhayet púrva-káryaṃ tu kṛita-kárya-vinirṇayaḥ* (probably for *nirṇayam*). This Çloka containing, as far as its meaning can be ascertained, an advice to claimants how to proffer their claim (see for a similar specification of the requirements of a claim Ragh. 12), has not been translated, as it comes in very awkward, and is wanting in a quotation of this whole passage contained in the Víramitrodaya. It is evidently a gloss added by some one to the term *púrvaváda*, which occurs in the preceding Çloka.

27. L *guṇáḥ sasa sahya-vahner ivárchishaḥ*. B *guṇáḥ sapta sapta*, etc. I have translated the latter reading; *sahya-vahni* would be "a strong fire."

35a. MSS. *yukti-yukto vidharmataḥ* for *yukti-yukto vidhiḥ smṛitaḥ*. 35b. MSS. *abhidíyate* for *avahíyate*.

36. Apparently as a gloss to the last words of this Çloka: *chauraç cháyáty achauratám* half a Çloka: *achauraç chauratáṃ yáto maṇḍávyo* (for *dáṇḍavyo?*) *vyavaháratah* has been inserted in the MSS. before the next Çloka, which is quoted in the Víramitrodaya. It has not been translated.

37. MSS. *stríshu çatrau cha balibhir antar veçmani*

*rátṛishu:* corrected into *stríshu rátrau bahir grámát antar veçmany arátishu* according to Víram.

46b. MSS. *'nyathá kurvann utkráman daṇḍabhág bhavet* for *'nyathá kurvann ásedhá daṇḍabhág bhavet* Mit. and Vír., *utkraman* being evidently a gloss, which was inserted in the text by mistake, and afterwards took the place of *násedhá*, which was left out in order to restore the metre.

51b. MSS. *nápakshát pakshántaraṃ* (B *nányat pakshántaraṃ*) *gachchan púrvát pakshát sa híyate.* Both readings are strongly corrupted, the reading of L even more than that of B, as *nápakshát* seems to be abbreviated from *nányat* for metrical reasons, and as the Çloka still contains one syllable too much. I read: *yas tu pakshántaraṃ gacchet púrvát pakshát sa híyate,* since *yas tu* could have been easily altered into *na*, in order to make the beginning of this Çloka agree with the opening words of the two hemistichs of 50 and the first hemistich of 52.

55. *nirṇikte vyavaháre tu pramáṇam aphalam bhavet* || *likhitaṃ sákshiṇo vápi púrvam aveditaṃ na cet.* The first hemistich is wanting in the MSS. and has been supplied from the Mit. and the Vir.; in the second, the reading of the MSS. *na cet* is supported by Mit. Vír. has *na vá.*

59b. Read *na hi játu* (MSS. *yátu*) *viná daṇḍaṃ kaçchid durge* (Vír. *márge*) *'vatishṭhate.*

2.

1.—Vír. 37. Col. Ess. i, 516. 2.—Ragh. 4. Vír. 37. Col. Ess. i, 514. 3.—Col. Ess. ibid. 6.—Col. l. c. 522. 7, 8.—Vír. 36. Col. l. c. 514. 9.—Manu 8, 16. Col. l. c. 522. 10.—Manu 8, 17. Col. l. c. 523. 11.—Col. l. c. 522. 12.—Col. l. c. 523. 13.—Manu, 8,

14. Col. ibid. 14.—Manu, 8, 15. Col. ibid. 15.—Manu, 8, 12. Col. ibid. 16.—Manu 8, 13. Col. 516. 17.—Col. 523. 18.—Ragh. 6. M. 8, 18. Mit. 359. 21.—Col. 522. 22.—Vír. 32. Col. 523. 23.—Mit. 126. Col. 523. 24.—Col. 523.

8b.—11 is omitted in B without apparent reason. It is true that 9 and 10 belong to Manu also, but so do 13, etc., and several Çlokas in other chapters; and other Dharmaçástras, as, for instance, Vishṇu, have a far greater number of Çlokas in common with Manu than Nárada.

3.

1.—Mit. 62. Vír. 292. Viv. 1. 2.—Mit. 75. Viv. 15. Vír. 341. Col. Dig. i, 5, clxix. May. v, 4, 14. 3.—Vír. 355. Viv. 18. Dig. i, 5, clxxxi. May. v, 4, 20. 4.—Mit. 78. Vír. 342. Dig. i, 5, cic. 5, 6.—Vír. 340. Dig. i, 5, clxxxviii. 6.—Mit. 74. 8, 9.—Vír. 358. May. v, 4, 11. 10.—Dig. l. c. 12.—Vír. 353. Dig. i, 5, cxciv. 13.—Vír. 352. Dig. i, 5, cxci. 14.—Vír. 342. Viv. 15. Dig. ib. clxxv. May. v, 4, 13. *16.—Dig. ibid. clxxxiii. *17.—Ibid. ccix. 17a.—Vír. 353. Viv. 19. *18.—Vír. 355. Dig. i, 5, ccxiii. *19.—Viv. 19. Dig. ibid. ccix. 20.—Vír. 355. Dig. ccxxv. May. v, 4, 20. 21.—Mit. 78. Dig. ibid. ccxxvii. May. v, 4, 19. Vír. 348. 24.—Viv. 19. Vír. 347. Dig. i, 5, ccxxiii. 25.—Mit. 79. Vír. 345. Viv. 17. Dig. i, 5, clxxii. May. v, 4, 19. 26.—Mit. 77. Vír. 347. Viv. 19. Dig. i, 5, ccxxi. 31, 32.—Vír. 126. —Vír. 340. Mit. 74. 33a.—Dig. i, 5, clxxxviii. Vír. 126. 33b.—Ragh. 47. Vír. 127. *35–39.—Ragh. 64. Vír. 127. 37, 38a.—Vír. 341. 40.—Vír. 128. 41–43.—Vír. 126. 42, 43.—Ragh. 63. 47, 49.—Dig. i, 4, xxvii. Both MSS. insert the following hemistich after 13 : *deyaṃ bháryá-kṛitam ṛiṇam bhartrá, putreṇa mátṛikam.* It has not been translated, as it is apparently a later addition: such a rule as this would be impossible in a Hindu Law Book, and it contradicts flatly the rule given in 19. This hemistich occurs as the first part of a Çloka ascribed to Kátyáyana, Vír. 356, which contains a rule of similar import as the 13th Çloka, to illustrate which some one appears to have inserted it.

16. B *aviyutaiḥ,* L *aviyuḥtaiḥ,* evidently for *aviyuktaiḥ.*

17. B *yadyayetád* (L *yadyupetád*) *ṛite yad vá saha tábhyáṃ kṛitaṃ bhavet:* probably for *pratipannád ṛite,* see Mit. 72; *upetya* may have been added in order to explain *pratipannád,* and was afterwards inserted in the text instead of it and corrupted.

18. L *ye vá tad ṛiktham ápadyeyatáṛiktham ṛiṇaṃ tataḥ,* corrected into *yá vá tad ṛiktham ápadyed yatohyṛiktham, ṛiṇaṃ tataḥ,* partly according to B, partly according to Vír.

19. L and Vír. *kuṭumbártho hi dustaraḥ.* B *kuṭumbaṃ ca tatháçrayam,* corrected into *kuṭumbaṃ hi tadáçrayam* according to Dig. l. c.

20b. *tasyádhanaṃ haret sarvaṃ niḥsvayáḥ putra eva tu* is erroneously repeated in the MSS. after the first hemistich of 21.

34. L *svegṛihe,* B *sve gṛihe gṛihe,* probably for *sve gṛihe gṛihí.*

The second hemistich of 36: *svatantras tu tatra gṛihí yasya tat syát kramágatam* has been supplied from Ragh. In the quotation of this passage in the Vír. it is wanting, as in the MSS.

39. MSS. *tayorapi pitá çrímán,* corrected into *çreyán* according to Ragh.

4.

1.—Vír. 105. 4.—Ragh. 50. Vír. 207. 5.—Ragh. 48. Vír. 209. *6.—Ragh. 46. Vír. 209. Manu, 8, 147. *7.—Vír. 211. 8.—Manu, 8, 148. 9.—Vír. 220. Manu, 8, 149. 11.—Ragh. 53. 13, 14.—Mit. 48. Vír. 204. May. ii, 2, 1. 16.—Mit. 41. Vír. 206. May. ii, 2, 2. 18.—Vír. 204. *20.—Ragh. 52. Vír. 204. 22.—Mit. 54. Ragh. 51. 23.—Mit. 50. Vír. 206. 26.—Mit. 102. Vír. 155. 27.—Yájnavalkya 2, 23. 28.—Vír. 293. Viv. 1. Dig. i, 1, ii. 29a.—Viv. 4. 29-31.—Mit. 63. Dig. i, 2, xxxvi. 32.—Vír. 299. Viv. 8. Dig. i, 2, xlv. 36.—Mit. 64. Vír. 301. Viv. 6. 36, 37.—Viv. 7. Dig. i, 2, lviii. *39, 40.—Mit. 79. Vír. 349, 356. Viv. 20. Dig. i, 5, ccxxxi. May. v, 4, 21. *41.—Vír. 357. D. i, 6, cclxxxvii. 42.—Vír. 358. Dig. i, 6, cclxxxiv. May. v, 4, 10. 44.—Mit. 87. Dig. i, 1, xxii. 45b.—Dig. i, 4, cxliii. *47.—Vír. 324. Dig. i, 4, cxliii. 49.—Yàjnavalkya 2, 55. 50.—Mit. 84. Vír. 328. Dig. i, 4, clxi. 51.—Mit. 87. Viv. 10. 51, 52a.—Vír. 305. 51, 52.—Dig. i, 3, lxxxi. 52b, 53a.—Vír. 306. Viv. 10, Dig. i, 3, lxxxi. 53b.—Mit. 90. Viv. 11. Dig. i, 3, lxxxiii. 54.—Vír. 311. Viv. 11. Dig. i, 3, xcv. 55.—Manu 8, 168. 56.—Vír. 359. Dig. i, 6, cclxxiv. 57.—Vír. 338. Viv. 21. Dig. i, 6, ccl. 59.—Mit. 119. Ragh. 43. Vír. 190. Dig. i, 1, xiii. May. ii, 1, 5. *60.—Mit. 123. Vír. 193. 61.—Mit. 122. Vír. 190. *62.—Ragh. 43. 64.—Mit. 90. Vír. 311. 65.—Ragh. 43. Vír. 200. 67.—Mit. 125. Ragh. 43. Vír. 196. May. ii, 1, 9. 69, 71.—Ragh. 43.

1b. B *sídanti cha pramáṇáni pramáṇair avyavasthitaiḥ*. L . . . *purushasyá' parádhataḥ*. The former reading has been preferred, as being more appropriate and supported by the Vír.

9.—L *rájasva-çrotriyayor dravyam.* B . . . *çrotriyor.* The original reading then appears to be *rája-çrotriyayor dravyam,* whereas Manu and the Vír. l. c. have: *rájasvaṃ çrotriyasvaṃ cha.*

19. B, L *áhate vá 'bhiyuktaḥ san ná 'rthánám uddharet padam,* I have corrected into *áhatena* and translated accordingly.

20a. B, L *pitrá púrvatareṇa vá,* altered into *púrvatarais tribhiḥ* according to Ragh. and Vir., since it is not possession held by the father alone, but only possession held by three former generations including the father, which confers proprietary right.

21a. L *kálavashṭaddha-yáchitam.* B. *kálaváshṭadhvayáchitam* (sic), conjecturally altered into *kálánváhitayáchitam*: though this enumeration comprises six kinds; on deposits see iii. head of dispute, 7.

After 30a the following hemistich: *bhinded arthaparímáṇam kaleneharṇikasya yat* is inserted in the MSS., but not found in the quotations of this whole passage in the Mit., etc. It interrupts the connexion between 30a and 30b, and is apparently a gloss added in order to state the occasions when loans are made on *káritá* interest, namely, in times of distress.

34. B *rapuṇaḥ.* L *puṇaḥ,* instead of *ṭrapuṇaḥ* "tin": see Vasishṭha, quoted Vír. 299.

39a. *na chásti saḥ* according to B and the quotations; L *na vásti saḥ.*

47a. L *ṛiṇishv apratikurvatsu prasavaivá 'pi yáchite.* B *prasaveváyáchite*: makes no sense and has been altered into *pratyaye vá 'pi hápite* according to Vír. and Dig.

60a. MSS. *vyaktávikriti-lakshaṇam,* Mit. and Vír. *vyaktádhividhi-lakshaṇam.* The latter reading has been preferred, being more appropriate and better intelligible than the former, which might be translated: *"a document*, which has evidently not been altered."

71a. MSS. *hatonmishṭa.* Ragh. *kritonmṛishṭa*: corrected into *hṛitonmṛishṭa*, cf. 67.

5.

1.—Vír. 142. May. ii, 3, 1. 3.—Mit. 98. Vír. 143. 4.—Mit. ibid. Vír. ibid. 6.—Mit. 99. Vír. 144. 7a.—Ibid. *9.—Vír. 149. May. ii, 3, 6. 10.—Vír. 158. 11.—Mit. 101. 11–13.—Vír. 151 (where 17b is inserted by mistake). *13b, 14a.—Mit. 102. 14.—Ragh. 31. Vír. 152. 15.—Mit. 101. Ragh. 30. Vír. 152. 17.—Mit. 102. May. ii, 3, 7. 18.—Mit. 102. Vír. 154. 19.—Mit. 113. 22.—Mit. 117. Vír. 184. 24.—Ragh. 40. Vír. 146. 25–27.—Vír. 147. 28.—Vír. ibid. 29–32.—Vír. 223. 30–32.—Ragh. 54. 33.—Manu, 8, 64. 35b.–45.—Vír. 157, 158. 46.—Ragh. 27. 47.—Vír. 160. *48.—Ragh. 29. Vír. 150. 49–52.—Vír. 166. May. ii, 3, 13. 53.—Vír. 161. May. ii, 3, 8. 54.—Vír. 162. Manu, 8, 72. 55.—Vír. 183. *56, 57.—Manu, 8, 120, 121. 58.—Mit. 105. Vír. 168. May. ii, 3, 16. 59.—Manu, 8, 113. 60.—Mit. 107. Vír. 169. 61.—Manu, 8, 81. 62.—Manu, 8, 93. 64.—Manu, 8, 89. 70.—Manu, 8, 97. 72.—Manu, 8, 98. 73.—Manu, 8, 99. 90.—Ragh. 41. 94b–97.—Vír. 172. 98–102a.—Vír. 224. 102.—Ragh. 55. Vír. 225, 227. *103.—Manu, 8, 115. 104.—Mit. 39. Ragh. 57. Vír. 113. 105.—Vír. 113. 108, 109.—Vír. 287. 110, 111.—Vír. 226. 113b, 114.—Vír. 239 (with several different readings). 114b, 115.—Vír. 235. 117.—Mit. 134. Vír. 240. *123b, 124a.—Vír. 249. 126.—Vír. 252. 127.—Vír. 250. 129.—Mit. 145. Vír. 253.

7b. In this place there is either a hemistich too much or too little in the MSS. I have decided for the former alternative and ejected the words: *kulíná ṛijavaḥ çuddháḥ janmataḥ karmato 'rthataḥ*, partly because they seem to be taken from Yájn. 2, 68, 69, partly because they are almost synonymous with part of the next Çloka, as the following translation will show: "*they shall be* of good families, honest, and pure as regards their descent, actions, and property."

9a. MSS. *çreshṭhavargeshu varginaḥ*. Vír. and May. *sveshu vargeshu*, which latter reading has been translated.

After 26a the following Çloka is erroneously inserted in both MSS. *átmanaiva likhejjánañ jánaṃstv anyair na lekhayet* || *ashthamád vatsarat siddhir tadvad gúḍhasya sákshiṇaḥ*. It is a perfectly unmeaning repetition, in its first part, of 24b, in its second part, of 26a.

27a. L *athaválaniyamo na dridhaḥ sákshiṇam prati*, evidently corrupted from B and Vír. *athavá kálaniyamo*.

40. MSS. *saunikáḥ*, altered into *múlikáḥ* according to Vír.

43. It seems as if half a Çloka was wanting either here or above after 35a.

48. MSS. *asákshy eko'pi sákshitve* "he is no witness," for *sa sákshy* (Ragh. *bhavaty eko*) Vír. 150; see also the parallel passages quoted in the latter work.

56A. MSS. *ajnánád bálabhávách cha sákshí yady anṛitaṃ vadet*. "If a witness speaks falsely through ignorance or inattention." But this sentence is not continued, and the three following hemistichs being taken from Manu 8, 120, 121, I have ejected this hemistich and substituted Manu 8, 121b, for it, which partly agrees with it.

61. Consists of three hemistichs in my translation; the first of these might also have been treated as a detached one.

After 64a, 63b and 64b is erroneously repeated in the MSS., only with one slight modification, *vivaçaḥ* for *andhaḥ*.

104. MSS. *na chárttim ichchhati* for *ṛichchhati* Manu l. c..

6.

2b, 3.—Mit. 151. 4a.—Mit. 151. Vír. 256. 10, 11. —Mit. 149. Vír. 261 (where these two Çlokas are ascribed to Pitámaha).

7a. MSS. *maṇḍaláni yathákramam* has been altered into *m. çaṇair gachchhet,* as it is necessary to have a verb here, neither of the two preceding Çlokas containing one. The expression *çaṇair gachchhet* occurs in a passage ascribed to Nárada, Vír. 264, see also the parallel passage of Yájn. with the commentary of the Mitákshará, Mit. 150.

7.

4.—Mit. 156. Vír. 268. 10.—Vír. 272. 14.—Vír. 270.

6. MSS. *puni,* evidently for *puṃsi.*

14. Vír. *tasmát' toye viçeshataḥ* || *kriyate dharmatattva-jnair dúshitánáṃ viçodhanam.* This is no doubt the correct reading of this passage; owing to a clerical error, which is easily explained, the MSS. have: *tasmát toyaṃ viçeshataḥ* || *tasmát toyaṃ samabhavad dharmatas trátum arhasi.*

8.

3.—Mit. 159. Vaijayantí ad Vishnu 13, 2. Vír. 274.

5a. MSS. *vishasya tu palárddh* (B *paladdh*) *árddha-sthita-bhagaṃ ghṛitaplutam.* The text being strongly corrupted here, I have substituted for this hemistich a translation of a whole Çloka of similar import, which is quoted as Nárada's Mit. 160, Vír. 274, and in Raghunandana's *Divyatatva* (ii, p. 343 of the Serampore edition of his *Tatvas*).

9.

1b, 2a.—Vír. 278. 6.—Mit. 162. Vír. 237 (with several different readings).

ii. head of dispute.

1.—Viv. 23. Vír. 361. Dig. ii, 1, iii. May. vi, 1. 2b.—Vír. 361. 3.—Viv. 23. Dig. ii, 1, xv. *4, 5.—* Viv. 25. Vír. 365. Dig. ii, 1, xxxvi. 6.—Vír. 132. 7. —Mit. 96. Vír. 363. Viv. 28. Dig. ii, 1, xxii. 8.—Mit. 98. Viv. 25. Dig. ii, 1, xi. May. vi, 1. 9.—Dig. ibid.

iii.

1.—Vír. 383. Dig. ii, 3, i. May. viii, 1. 2.—Dig. ii, 3, iii. 3.—Vír. 384. Dig. ii, 3, iv. *4.—Vír. 384. Dig. ibid. vii. 5.—Dig. ibid. xiii. 6.—Vír. 386. Viv. 29. Dig. ibid. xvi. 7.—Viv. 30. Dig. ibid. xix. 8.—Vír. 388. Dig. ibid. xxviii. 9, 10.—Vír. 389. Viv. 33. 9, 11.—Dig. ibid. xliii. 14.—Viv. 30. Dig. ibid. xx. 15. —Viv. ibid. Dig. ibid. 16.—Viv. 31. Dig. ibid.

iv.

1.—Mit. 258. Vír. 392. Viv. 35. Dig. ii, 4, ii. May. ix, 1. 2.—Mit. 259. Vír. Viv. Dig. May. ibid. 3.—Viv. 35. Dig. ibid. *3b.—Mit. 261. Vír. 397. May. iv, 6. 4, 5.—Mit. 260. Vír. 392. Viv. 36. Dig. ibid. iv. May. ix, 2. *7–10.—Mit. 261. Vír. 398. Viv. 39. 7.—Dig.

* 4 of the MSS. is an unintelligible extract from the two Çlokas on the same subject quoted in the Dharmanibandhas. The latter have therefore been substituted for it.

ibid. l. 8, 9.—Dig. ibid. liii. 10.—Dig. ibid. lxv. 8–10—May. ix, 6. 11.—Dig. ii, 4, lxvii. (with different readings). 11a.—Vír. 393. Viv. 41.

3. MSS. *dattam ashṭavidham* for *saptavidham*: only seven valid gifts are enumerated in 7.

v.

1.—Mit. 266. Vír. 400. Dig. iii, x, ii. May. x, 1. 2.—Dig. ibid. iii. 2–7.—Mit. 267. Vír. 401. 2, 3.—Vír. 41. 3, 5,—Dig. iii, 1, vi. vii. xxvi. 8.—Vír. 402. Viv. 41. Dig. iii, 1, ix. 14.—Vír. 402. Dig. iii, 1, 9. 15–19.—Mit. 272. Viv. 42. 15, 16.—Vír. 403. Dig. ibid. xvii. 17.—Vír. 409. Dig. ibid. xix. 18.—Vír. 403. Dig. ibid. xx. 19.—Vír. 404. Dig. ibid. xxii. 20, 21.—Viv. 42. Dig. ibid. xxiii. 21, 22.—Vír. 405. 21.—Mit. 267. 22—Viv. 43. Dig. ibid. xxv. 23.—Dig. xxvi. 24–26.—Mit. 268. Vír. 408. Viv. 43. Dig. ibid. xix. May. x, 5. 27, 28.—Viv. 44. May. x, 6. 27.—Vír. 409. Dig. xxxv. 28.—Mit. 269. Vir. 410. Dig. xlii. 29.—Mit. 270. Viv. 44. Dig. liii. 29a, 30a, 31, 32, 34.—Vír. 410. 30a, 31, 32.—Mit. 270. May. x, 7. 30.—Viv. 44. Dig. xlv. 31.—Viv. 45. Dig. xlvi. 32.—Viv. 45. Dig. xlvii. 33.—Viv. 43. Vír. 407. 34.—Viv. 45. Dig. xlviii. 35.—Vír. 409. Viv. 44. Dig. xxxv. May. x, 6. *36.—Mit. 269. Viv. 44. Vír. 411. Dig. xl. 37.—Mit. 271. Vír. 406. Viv. 46. Dig. lvi. May. x, 2. 38.—Vír. 411. Viv. 44. Dig. ixl. May. x, 8. *39.—Viv. 46, Dig. li. Manu 8, 416. *40–42.—Vír. 412. Viv. 45. Dig. l. May. x, 10.

vi.

1—Vír. 413. Dig. iii, 1, lxi. May. xi, 1. 2.—Mit. 277. 2, 3.—Vír. 414. Viv, 48. Dig. iii, 1, lxii. 4.—Dig. iii, 1, lxx. *5.—Vír. 416, Viv. 49. May. xi, 4. Dig. iii, 1, lxxii. 6A.—Dig. ibid. xcii. 7.—Vír. 419. 7, 8a.—

Dig. ibid. lxxxix. 8b—Vír. 418. 9—Mit. 279. Vír. 418. Dig. ibid. lxxxii. 10—Vír. 442. Viv. 51. Dig. iii, 4, iii. 11—Vír. 442. Viv. 52. Dig. iii, 4, v. *12, 13—Vír. 444. Dig. iii, 4, xi. 14—Manu 8, 232, etc. 15—Manu 8, 235, etc. *16.—Manu 8,233, etc. *17—Viv. 53. Dig. iii, 4, xvii. 18, 19—Vír. 422. Viv. 50. 18—Dig. iii, 1, xcv. 20–22—May. xi, 7. 20–21—Vír. 420. Dig. iii, 1, ic. *22—Vír. 421. (where, however, the new Calc. ed. puts erroneously *gṛihítur á* for "*gṛihitur na*"). Dig. iii, 1, civ.

7a. MSS. *adadan kárayitvá tu dháaṇḍa-dnyá-dhikaṃ dhanam*. This hemistich yielding no proper sense, another has been substituted for it, which is quoted in the Vír. and Dig. as first hemistich to 7b.

16a. The Viv., where this Çloka is also quoted, p. 52, exhibits a slightly different reading, which is the one translated by Col. Dig. iii, 4, vii.

vii.

1—Mit. 253. Vir. 374. Dig. ii, 2, iii. 2—Mit. 254. Vír. 375. 2b.—Dig. ii, 2, xxvi. 3—Viv. 27. Vír. 375. Dig. ii, 2, xxxviii. 4—Viv. 28. Dig. ii, 2, li. 5—Dig. ii, 2, xxxi.

viii.

1—Vír. 437. Dig. iii, 3, 17. May. xiii, 2, 1. 2, 3—Vír. 437. Dig. iii, 3, ii. iii. 4—Vír. 437. Viv. 55. Dig. iii, 3, 18. *5—Vír. 437, 438. Viv. 55. Dig. ibid. xix. 6—Vír. 439. Viv. 56. Dig. ibid. xxvii. 7, 8—Vír. 440. Dig. ibid. xxx. xxxiii. 9—Vír. 438. Dig. ibid. xxxiv. May. xiii, 2, 3. *10—Vír. 441. Viv. 46. Dig. ibid. xx. May. xiii, 2, 4. 11, *12—Viv. 57. Dig. ibid. xxxviii.

ix.

1—Mit. 263. Vír. 433. Dig. iii, 3, iv. May. xiii, 1, 1. 2, 3—Mit. 263. Vír. 435. Viv. 58. Dig. iii, 3, v. May. xiii, 1, 3. 4—Mit. 264. Viv. 58. Vír. 433, 435. Dig. ibid. x. 5, 6—Vír. 433. Viv. 38, 58. Dig. ibid. xiii. May. xiii, 1, 3. 7—Vír. 436. Viv. 58. Dig. ibid. xvi, May. xiii, 1, 3. 8, *9 (resp. 9a)—Vír. 372. Dig. iii, 3, li. May. vi, 8. 16—Vír. 434. Viv. 58. Dig. iii, 3, x.

x.

1—Mit. 272. Vír. 423. Dig. iii, 2, iii. May. xii, 1. 2—Vír. 425. Viv. 53. Dig. iii, 2, x. May. xii, 3. 3—Vír. 430. Dig. iii, 2, xi. 4—Vír. 430. Dig. iii, 2, xxviii. 5—Dig. ibid. xxv. *6—Vír. 430. Dig. ibid. xvi. 7—Vír. 431. Dig. ibid. xxviii.

xi.

1—Vír. 451. 3—Vír. 456. 7—Mit. 240. May. xv, 4. 8b—Mit. 241. 9—Mit. 238. Vír. 458. Viv. 60. May. xv, 2. 10—Mit. ibid. Vír. 458. Viv. 60. 11—Vír. 460. Viv. 61. *15—Vír. 464. May. xv, 8. 17—Vír. 467. May. xv, 13. *18—Mit. 244. Vaijayantí *ad* Vishṇu 5, 15. *20-22—Vír. 468. 20—May. xv, 13. 20, 21—Mit. 244. 23—Vír. 469. Viv. 67. 24—Vír. 470. Viv. ibid. *26—Vír. 470. Viv. 65. 28—Vír. 446. Dig. iii, 4, xxx. 29a—Vír. 450. 29—Viv. 67. Col. Dig. ibid. xlix. 30—Vír. 449. Dig. ibid. lv. *31 Mit. 247. Vír. 448. Dig. ibid. xlvii. 33—Viv. 67. Dig. ibid. xlvi. 34—Mit. 248. Dig. ibid. xlvii. 35, 36—Vír. 449. Viv. 68. Dig. ibid. lii. 37—Mit. 249. Vír. 450. Viv. 67. Dig. ibid. li. 38—Dig. ibid. 39—Mit. 249. Dig. iii, 4, xxvii. *40—Dig. iii, 4, xxxiii.

6 contains no verb, and I have supplied one in my

translation conformably to a remark made in the Viv. 60; it seems more likely, however, that a whole Çloka is missing here. The text of this Çloka itself is corrupted in B, and the readings of L have been followed.

After 33 both MSS. very improperly insert the following Çloka: *nashṭá bhagná cha lagná cha vṛishabhaḥ kṛita-lakshaṇaḥ || proktaṃ tuchhinnanáśáyáṃ vasantyáṃ tu chaturguṇam.* It consists of two separate hemistichs, the first of which refers to some further cases, in which trespasses of cattle are not finable, whereas the second is a more awkward variation of 33a. The first hemistich also contains a repetition, since *nashṭá* is synonymous with *ágantukí* "a stray" in 32. Neither of the two hemistichs is quoted elsewhere, and being apparently later additions, they have not been translated.

After 36 another hemistich had to be omitted: *sasyaṃ vináçayed gauç chen, na daṇḍaḥ kalpito yataḥ* (probably for *kalpiteyo 'taḥ*) because it wholly interrupts the connexion between the two halves of Çloka 36, and is not found in any of the quotations of this whole passage (see above). It is evidently a gloss.

xii.

1—Mit. 351. Vír. 513. 28—Manu 9, 47. 34—Manu 8, 225. 35—Dig. iv, 4, clxxxii. 46-54—Mit. 77. Dig. iv, 4, clviii. 47, 50—Viv. 19. 55—Dig. v, 5, cccxliii. 57—Manu 9, 54. 58—Vír. 604. Dig. v, 4, ccxxxix. 59—Dig. v, 4, cclxvi. 62, 63—Viv. 109. *66—Manu 8, 358. 66, 67—Viv. 110. 69—Vír. 506. 72—Viv. 113. 73-75—Mit. 342. Vír. 507. Viv. 118. May. xix, 8. *76—Viv. 120. 77—Viv. ibid. *78,

*79—Mit. 346. Vír. 510. *80b–83—Dig. iv, 4, cxlvii, 1–4. *86, 87—ibid. 6, 7. *90—Dig. iv. i, lxiii. *91 —Vír. 520. Dig. iv, 1, lxxxi. 92—Dig. iv, 1, lxiii. 93, 94—Dig. iv, 1, lxiv. 95—Vír. 520. Dig. iv, 1, lix.

10 — L *reyasyápsuplavatevírjandimútraṃchaphenilam.* B. *retasyoplavatenásuhládim.* I suspect the true reading to be *ápsu yasya plavate viḍ reto mútraṃ cha phenilam*: see the signs of *impotency* as enumerated by Kátyáyana, Dig. v, 5, cccxxx. The readings of the MSS. make no sense at all.

Owing to a palpable mistake of the copyist, half a Çloka, literally agreeing with the first half of 33, has been inserted after 31a in both MSS.

40. B. *rákshasonavarostasmát.* L. *rákshaso navarasyát,* probably for *'navaras tu syát*—if the term *anavara* (which is wanting in B. R.'s Dictionary) can have the meaning I have assigned to it: 'the one immediately preceding the last in rank, *or* the last but one.'

46—53. The second *svairiṇí,* in the enumeration given in the Mitákshará and in Colebrooke's Digest, ranks as second among the *punarbhú* wives in the MSS., and the second *punarbhú* of the Mit. and Dig. is in the MSS. mentioned as the last of the *svairiṇís.* The order observed in the Mit. and Dig. is supported by a quotation in the Vivádachintámani, which defines the fourth *svairiṇí* in the same manner as the two before-mentioned works. But if regard is paid to the remark that "the first (in this emuneration) are more despicable than those subsequently mentioned" (Çl. 54) the arrangement given in the MSS. seems preferable. Other slight deviations from the Mit. and Colebrooke's translation were necessitated by different readings; the reading *práptá déçád"* having come from a different country," in 52 is recommended by the context and supported by the Mit. and Viv. Colebrooke has for it "having had a protector assigned to her."

78.—*nishkásiní* Mit. and Vír., both MSS. *nisvá-miní.*

79.—L. *gamyá api hi nopeyá yatas tásya parigraháḥ.* B. *yátas tá syuḥ parigraháḥ.* Mit., Vír. better *gamyásv api hi nopeyád yat táḥ para-parigraháḥ.*

83. "A younger—wife" has been supplied from Colebrooke's Dig. l.c., since evidently half a Çloka is wanting here in the Sanskrit text.

87. Between and after the second half-Çloka the words *snátá puṃsavane çuçiḥ . . . kṛite garbhe tathaiva sá,* which, being arranged in inverse order, would form another half-Çloka, are found in the Sanskrit text. I have omitted them, because no corresponding phrase is found in the Digest l. c., and, chiefly, because they disturb the connexion.

90. Both MSS. *atonyaṃ tyajator* (B. *tyajato*) *nágaḥ syád* corrected into *anyonyam tyajator ágah* according to Colebrooke's translation l. c.

94. MSS. *kurvann evaṃ na doshabhák* for *sa dosha-bák,* corrected according to Col. l. c.

102. L. *shaj janma,* B. *saj janma* apparently stands for *yaj janma.*

Of the rejected half-Çlokas, which are inserted before and after 106a in the MSS., the first: *saṃskáraç cha rúpákádyás* (B. *ádyá*) *tesháṃ triḥsaptakoshṭataḥ* makes no sense and interrupts the connexion; the second *ambashṭhaugrau tathá putráv evaṃ kshatriya-vaiçyayoḥ* (cf. Manu x, 8. 9) is likewise inappropriate as the two castes mentioned in it do not belong to the "same" (*evaṃ*) category of the *Anantaras,* and as the descent of the *Ambashṭha* is stated once more, and more correctly, in the following half-Çloka.

xiii.*

1.—Col. Dig. v, 1, 5; Mit. I, 1, 5. May. iv, 3, 1. 2.—Col. Dáy. I, 3; Mit. II, 11, 18; Dig. v, 9, ccccixi. May. iv, 10, 20. 3.—Col. Dáy. I, 32; Mit. I, 2, 7; Dig. v, 2, xcviii. May. iv, 4, 2. 4.—Col. Dáy. II, 81; Dig. v, 1, xxiv. 5.—Col. Dáy. iii, 1, 1; Dig. v. i, 11. 6.—Col. Dáy, vi, 1, 12; Dig. v, 6, cccliii; Mit. i, 1, 19. May. iv, 7, 11. 7.—Col. Dig. v, 5, cccliii. 8.—Col. Dáy. iv, 1, 4; Dig. v, 9, ccccixix. 9.—Col. Dáy. ibid.; Dig. v, 9, DIV. 10.—Col. Dáy. vi, 1, 14; Mit. i, 1, 8; Dig. v, 5, ccclvii. May. iv, 4, 9. 11.—Col. Dáy. vi, 1, 16; Dig. v, 5, cccli. May. iv, 7, 10. 12.—Col. Dáy. ii, 35; Mit. i, 5, 7; Dig. v, 1, xcvi. May. lv, 4, 12. 13.—Col. Dig. v, 1, lxxi. 14a.—Col. Dig. ibid.; 14b.—Dig. v, 3, cxli. 15.—Col. Dáy. ii, 75; Dig. v, 1, xxxii. May. iv, 14, 4. 16.—Col. Dáy. ii, 83; Mit. I, 2, 14 Dig. v, 1, xxviii. May. iv, 4, 6. 17.—Col. Dig. v, 4, cclxii. *18.—Vir. 607. 19, 20.—Col. Dig. v, 4, cccxlii. 21.—Col. Dáy. v, 13; Mit. ii, 10, 3; Dig. v, 4, cccxx. May. iv, 11, 3. 22.—Col. Dig. v, 4, cccxx. May. ibid. 23.—Col. Dig. v, 4, ccxlii. *24.—Col. Mit.

* The quotations from the Vír. and Viv. have been omitted in this chapter, on account of the great number of quotations from other works. The quotations from this chapter of Nárada which are contained in Dr. Burnell's translations of the Mádhavíya (Madras, 1868), and of Varadarájá's Vyavaháranirṇaya (Mangalore, 1872) have not been given, because the lists of quotations added to these works will easily enable the reader to find them.

ii, 1, 20; Dig. v, 8, ccccxxxiii. 25.—Col. Mit. ii, 1, 7; Dig. v, 8, ccccv. May. iv, 8, 6. 26.—Col. Mit. ibid.; Dig. ibid. May. ibid. 27.—May. iv, 9, 22 (wrong translation). 28, 29.—Vír. 515. Col. Dáy. xi, 1, 64; Dig. iv, 1, xiii.* 30.—Vír. 514. Col. Dig. iv, 1, iv. 31.—Col. Mit. ii, 1, 25; Baudháyana II, 2, 27. 32.—Col. Dáy. I, 47; Dig. v, 2, cxi. May. iv, 6, 2. 33. —Col. Dáy. iii, 2, 41; Dig. v, 3, cxxviii. 34.—Col. Dáy. iii, 2, 42; v, 3, cxxvii. 35.—Dig. v, 2, cviii. 36.—Col. Dáy. xiv, 1; Mit. ii, 12, 3; Dig. v, 6, ccclxxxi. May. iv, 7, 27. 37.—Col. Mit. ii, 12, 3; Dig. v, 6, ccclxxxvii. May. iv, 7, 28. 38.—Col. Dáy. xiv, 7. May. iv, 7, 34. Col. Dig. v, 6, ccclxxx. May. iv, 7, 38. 39.—Col. Dáy. xiv, 7; Mit. II, 12, 4; May. iv, 7, 34. Col. Dig. v, 6, ccclxxxvii. May. iv, 7, 34. 40.—Col. Dáy. xiv, 7; Dig. v, 6, ccclxxxvii. 41. not quoted. 42.—May. iv, 7, 36. 43.—Ibid. 43.—Col. Dáy. vii, 1. 45–47, 49.—Col. Dig. v, 4, clxxxviii. 47b. and 49.—Col. Dig. v, 4, ccc. 50.—Col. Dáy. iv, 2, 10. Dig. v, 8, ccccxix. 51.—Col. Dig. v, 8, ccccxlviii. May. iv, 8, 5. 52.—Col. Dig. ibid.; Mit. ii, 1, 28. May. ibid.

6b. *Lavibhájyáni.* B and Bühler's MS. *vibhajyáni*, corrected by him into *avibhaktáni.* But *avibhájyáni* appears to be the original reading.

11. Here again I have been obliged to deviate slightly from Bühler, who reads *vaidyovaidáya* and translates: "a learned man . . . to a learned co-heir." But L has *vaidyo 'vaidyáya,* from which reading B *vaidye vaidyáya* and the reading of Bühler's MS., *vaidya vaidyáya* appears to have been corrupted; L's is also the reading translated by Colebrooke.

14. B L *úḍhájáteshv,* Bühler's MS. *údhaṃ j.*, which

reading he alters into *gúḍhaṃjáteshv* ("born secretly"), but follows Colebrooke's translation "born from women legally married." The first reading is evidently the correct one.

18. MSS. *gúḍhamátṛikaḥ* for *múḍhamátṛikaḥ* reading of the Vír. 607, adopted, with full reason, by Bühler, and after him by Burnell Varad. p. 24 note.

21a. B *ghatitaḥ páṇḍur yaç cha syád aupapátikaḥ.* L *ghatitaḥ páṇḍur yapatitaḥ shaṇḍo yaç cha.* Corrected into *patitaḥ shaṇḍo yaç cha syád apapátritaḥ* partly according to Bühler, partly according to Colebrooke Dig. v, 5 cccxx. Dáy. v, 13, Mit. 2, 10. 3.

23. L supports Bühler's emendation of this Çloka (in his Dig. 354).

24b. Has been translated according to Bühler's emendation.

30a. Has been supplied with Bühler from Vír. 514. In L also there is a remark, in Colebrooke's hand, I think, in the margin, to the effect that "half a Çloka seems wanting here."

32. MSS. *ṛiṇí na syád yathá pitá,* supported by Colebrooke's translation. Bühler reads *ṛiṇí syád anyathá pitá.* See Burnell's remark, Var. 18 note.

34. MSS. *avaçya* for *avaçyaṃ* (Bühler).

42. L *pṛithi,* B *pṛithaḥ* for *pṛithak.* (Bühler).

xiv.

1.—Mit. 303. Vír. 498. Viv. 96. May. xviii, 1. 2a. —Ragh. 30. 3–6.—Mit. ibid. Vír. 498. 499. Viv. 96. May, xviii, 2. *7.—Mit. ibid. Vír. 499. Viv. 96. May. xviii, 16. 8.—Mit. 47, 304. Vír. 130. 499. Viv. 96. May, xviii, 16. 9, 10.—Mit. 47, etc. Vír. ibid. May. xviii, 6. 11.—Viv. 96. 12.—Vír. 490. Viv. 96. 13.—

Vír. 491. 14-*16.—Mit. 332. Vír. 489. May. xvii, 1. 17. —Mit. 325. Vír. 489. 19.—Viv. 93. May. xvii, 10. *19b.—Mit. 335. Vír. 498. 20.—Vír. 498. 21.—Viv. 90.

19b. MSS. *çaktau vadham upekshante* for *çaktáç cha yad upekshante,* Mit., Vír, May. The relative pronoun could not be wanting here, nor could the particle *cha* be omitted; besides it would be wholly inappropriate to mention the crime of murder (*vadha*) in this place.

25. *same 'dhvani dvayor yatra tena práyo* (L *prayo*) *çuchir* (=*açuchir* ?) *naraḥ* || *purvá-'pavádair dushṭo vá saṃsṛishṭo vá durátmabhiḥ.* My rendering of this Çloka is hypothetical, since the text of the first hemistich is unclear and apparently corrupted.

## XV.

1-3.—Mit. 285. Vír. 482. Viv. 69. *6.—Mit. 291. Vír. 470. May. xvi, 2, 1. 5, 6.—Mit. 292. Vír. 471. 7-14.—Mit. 292. 293. Vír. 471. 472. Viv. 78. 8, 9.—Mit. 24. 9.—Viv. 77. 17.—Manu 8, 269, etc. (deviating slightly). 18.—Manu 8, 274 (ditto). 21. —Vír. 488. May. xvi, 1, 6. 22-24.=Manu 8, 270-272. 25.—Vír. 476. Viv. 75; almost=M. 8, 279). *26-29.—M. 8, 281-284 (with several different readings). 30.—Vír. 488. 31.—Vír. 476. Viv. 75.

The agreement of 7-14 with the Çlokas quoted as Nárada's in the Dharmanibandhas is by no means perfect; but I have seen no reason for substituting the readings of those works to the readings found in the MSS., except in 10, where the reading of L *çaveshu* (B *sarishu*) *vadhavṛittishu* has been altered into *vyaṅgeshuv.*

xvi. (xvii.)

1.—Mit. 281. Vír. 718. 2.—Vír. ibid. 2a.—Mit. 283. 6. Mit. 284. Vír. 721. *7.—Vír. 721. Viv. 167. 8.—Vír. 718.

xvii. (xviii.)

*1–4.—Mit. 351. Vír. 722. 723. 9, 10.—Col. Ess. i, 521. 9.—Mit. 360. 10a. 11.—Vír. 724. 10, 11. Mit. 357. May. xxii, p. 167, 15a.—Manu 7, 20b.

9. MSS. *rájnádánaṃ kritaṃ bhavet* for *rájnájánaṃ* Mit. 360; the latter reading is supported by Colebrooke's translation also.

35a. L *agraṃ navaṃyaḥsasabhyam.* B *navaṃyaḥ-saptabhyam.* For *navabhyaḥ saptabhyo?* I have translated according to this conjecture; but it seems more likely, that the text is entirely corrupted here.

39 contains no verb, and I have supplied one from 40.

47. B L *bhúmyá yadbhága,* apparently for *bh.* (Instr. for Genit.) *shaḍbhágaṃ,* v. Manu 7, 130.

# GENERAL INDEX.

Roman numerals refer to heads of dispute, and Arabic numerals to chapters and verses. pp. refers to the page in the Preface and Notes. Int., Introduction.

# CORRIGENDA.

Page xxix, lines 13 and 20, *before* 1. *insert* Int. 1.

Page 2, line 11, *for Bṛhigu, read Bhṛigu.*

Page 5, line 8, *for* feet, and *read* feet, four bases, and

Page 7, line 3, *for* courses *read* eventualities.

Page 22, line 17, *for* butter *read* ghee.

Page 22, line 21, *for* refined sugar, human excrements, *read* gems, poison, human creatures.

Page 22, line 23, *for* leathern oil-bottles, *read* cloth made of wool.

Page 23, line 2, *for* grain, and the like, *read* for a corresponding quantity of grain.

Page 23, line 20, *for* 4. What, *etc. read* 4. Of those three kinds of evidence enumerated in order the first is superior to the one subsequently mentioned, but possession is more decisive than the two *others. Owing to a mistake, this Çloka has not been printed, and the numbering of the succeeding Çlokas from 5 to 15 has been altered accordingly* (*into* 4–14).

Page 27, lines 5 and 32, *for káyá and kaya, read káya.*

Page 74, lines 1, 2, *for* neither gain nor loss *read* the same gain and no loss.

Page 76, line 5, *for* channels, shrubs *read* valleys, hills.

Page 93, lines 5, 6, *for* Of these—order; *read* Of these, one is born in an inverse, and two in the direct, order;

Page 105, lines 5, 6, *for nishṭur, açlila,* and *tibra read nishṭhura, açlíla,* and *tívra.*

Page 105, lines 8–10, *for Nishṭhur,* etc. *read Nishṭhura . . . Açlíla . . . Tívra.*

Page 114, line 8, *for* displease *read* try to surpass.

Page 114, line 27, *for* but—tolls *read* and they shall be exempt from paying tolls.

Page 120, line 29, *after* 127 *insert* 33b. 35–39.—Dig. ii, 4, xv.

Page 120, line 31, *after* 126 *insert* 42.—Dig. ii, 4, liv.